CW00670107

TOUGH
OUTBACK

TOUGH
OUTBACK

MIKE BELLAMY

HarperCollins*Publishers*

HarperCollins*Publishers*
Australia • Brazil • Canada • France • Germany • Holland • India
Italy • Japan • Mexico • New Zealand • Poland • Spain • Sweden
Switzerland • United Kingdom • United States of America

First published in New Zealand in 2022
by HarperCollins*Publishers* (New Zealand) Limited
Unit D1, 63 Apollo Drive, Rosedale, Auckland 0632, New Zealand
harpercollins.co.nz

Copyright © Mike Bellamy 2022

Mike Bellamy asserts the moral right to be identified as the author of this work. This work
is copyright. All rights reserved. No part of this publication may be reproduced, copied,
scanned, stored in a retrieval system, recorded, or transmitted, in any form or by any means,
without the prior written permission of the publisher.

A catalogue record for this book is available from the National Library of New Zealand

ISBN 978 1 7755 4213 1 (pbk)
ISBN 978 1 7754 9244 3 (ebook)

Cover design by Lisa Reidy
Cover images by shutterstock.com and istockphoto.com
Typeset in Sabon LT Std by Kirby Jones
Printed and bound in Australia by McPherson's Printing Group

MIX
Paper from
responsible sources
FSC
www.fsc.org   FSC® C001695

This book is dedicated to all the hard-working men and women in the mining and construction industry, especially those who I've worked with over the years.

Contents

1

Out and about in Perth

I WAS DIGGING OUT a house site on a windy, grey day in 1989 when a car pulled up and this tanned, lean, long-haired bloke hopped out. It was my old mate, Sammy, who I hadn't seen in ages.

'How you going, Mike?' he asked.

'You haven't been a naughty boy spending time at Her Majesty's pleasure, have you, Sammy?'

'Bugger off, Mike. I've been behaving myself, thank you very much.' He laughed. 'I've been over in WA working up in the mines on a D11N impact dozer.'

The D11N was the largest dozer being produced by Caterpillar at the time, so I was surprised he'd been let loose on one. 'How did you get on that thing, mate? Did you tell a few porkies to get a start?'

'Easy as! That's why I'm here, Mike. The company I work for is screaming out for operators, so they asked me if I knew of anyone they can give a start.'

'Man, I'd love to give it a crack, but I've got no experience on large gear.'

'You don't need any, Mike. It's not rocket science. So, what d'you reckon? Keen?'

'My oath! Why not?'

It was to be the start of over 30 years working in the mining and construction industry in Australia.

* * *

On New Year's Day 1990, Sammy and I boarded a British Airways flight direct to Perth, Western Australia (WA). The plane was almost empty, with about eight people at most in the economy cabin.

We decided to have a bit of a New Year's celebration on the plane, so once we'd settled in, I pushed the buzzer to summon a flight attendant.

A female flight attendant wandered up from the back. 'Yes, sir?' she asked, with a look of resignation on her face. 'Will it be the same again? Two rums for you and two vodkas for your companion?'

Thanks ...' I said, as I leaned across and squinted, trying to read her name badge, 'umm, Claudia.'

About halfway into the flight, Sammy pressed the buzzer again. By that stage, neither of us was feeling any pain.

Claudia wheeled the drinks trolley up to us.

'How's it going, Claud? Two of the same, thanks, love,' Sammy said to her.

Claudia just looked at us, clicked on the drinks trolley's brakes and walked off. Over her shoulder as she went, she said, 'Help yourselves, gentlemen.'

'You're a legend, Claud,' Sammy called after her. You know, Mike?' – he looked at me – 'She'd have to be the nicest air hostess I've ever met.'

A few hours and a few more drinks later, we landed in Perth. Going through Customs, we both desperately tried to act as if we were sober. Thankfully, it worked even if I did stuff up by opening a broom cupboard door, thinking it was the exit. If it had been nowadays, every buzzer and alarm would have gone off when Sammy got scanned.

The airport had nice, cool air-conditioning, which I didn't notice until I walked out through the sliding doors. Boom! Outside I was met by a cloudless, deep-blue desert sky and a lovely 40-degree summer day. While we waited for a Swan taxi, sweat started rolling off me.

As we hopped in our taxi, the big, burly driver asked, 'How you going, cob? Where are you heading?'

'St George's Terrace, thanks, mate,' Sammy replied.

As we made our way into the city, I noticed lots of dry scrub, gumtrees and sand, which changed as we got closer to central Perth, when the landscape became like an oasis, with lush, green grass, ponds and parks everywhere and the Swan River sparkling like a jewel against the sandy foreshore.

We pulled up outside a hotel amid the old limestone buildings on St George's Terrace and, as I opened the taxi door – boom! – that heat hit me again, even though it was six o'clock in the evening.

'Man, it's a hot place, Sammy.'

'Mate, this is nothing!' He laughed. 'Wait till you get up to the bush – 45 degrees every day – and the flies will carry you away. You just wait!'

Having checked into the hotel and dropped off our gear, we decided to catch the train out to Fremantle, to have a bite to eat.

As we rolled along through the suburbs towards the coast, I noticed all the grand old Federation homesteads built of limestone, with their gracious bullnose verandahs and their backyards scattered with purple-flowering jacaranda trees.

As we passed the bustling container port and headed over the Swan River into Fremantle, the sun was setting over the Indian Ocean and the horizon glowed like it was on fire. What a sight.

My thoughts were interrupted by the train's intercom announcing our arrival into Fremantle. The train door slid open – boom! – there was that bloody heat again.

Walking up Market Street, with its mixture of convict-built colonial-era buildings and grand old Federation-style pubs, I felt like I'd gone back in time. I could almost feel the history of the port city. It was a novelty to sit outside on the footpath, drinking coffee at one of the many cafes that lined the main street, watching people stroll past on that warm summer's night. That night, I fell in love with the place.

* * *

Back at the hotel the next morning, I was woken by Sammy banging on my door. I opened my bloodshot, bleary eyes and, with my head pounding, I got up and opened the door.

Even though he looked like death warmed up, Sammy was clearly a man on a mission. 'Come on, Mike, I've got a mate down in his car who will give us a lift out to the mining company's HQ in Welshpool!'

I quickly got dressed and headed downstairs. Boom! The heat hit me once again as we stepped outside – and it was only 10 o'clock.

Sammy introduced me to Dino, who worked with him in the mines up at Mount Gibson. We shook hands and I got in the car.

Sammy piped up. 'We're just going for a bit of a drive first, Mike, out of the city.'

I thought, that's kind of Dino to show me around.

Well, we disappeared up some winding road out the back of Kalamunda. There was no air-con in the car so I was sitting in the 30-something-degree car while the other two were smoking something they shouldn't have been. To top it all off, I was dying of a hangover and ready to chuck.

Half an hour later, we pulled over in this discreet layby area, which was in the shade of some gumtrees. Dino turned the car off and I listened to the deafening noise of cicadas singing in the trees above us.

Dino quietly muttered to Sammy as an old Falcon pulled up right beside us. The driver wound his window down.

'Who's he?' the stranger asked, pointing at me.

'He's okay, he's my mate,' Sammy replied.

By then, I was wondering what the hell was going on.

Dino handed the stranger some cash out the window and the stranger handed him some white powder in tiny, wee bags. I hadn't realised Sammy was into shady dealings.

It turned out their plan was to take some of their purchase back to the mines to sell. They worked hard and played hard. Drugs and heavy drinking were rampant in the mines back in the early nineties.

I perked up a bit as we neared Welshpool – an industrial suburb about 10 kilometres southeast of the city centre, which was home to a number of mining companies. Parked out the front of the yards were rows of big dump trucks. As we drove along, I spotted triple-sevens, which were CAT's most popular workhorses, as well as a number of 785s and 773s. Then there were the big dozers – D9Ls, D10s and D11Ns – and there was even a few 651E motor scrapers, which were the biggest ones Caterpillar made. I was in heaven.

We passed Thiess and Leightons, Roche Brothers, AWP

Mining (also known as 'Australia's Worst Paid') and Henry Walker Eltin – most have gone now. We were headed for Kanny's, an opencut mining contractor that mainly specialised in drill and blast, and load and haul: a company that was eventually bought out by Macmahon Construction, which is still around today.

We pulled up outside Kanny's yard. Unlike the other companies, they seemed to have all the older model machines (old dungers) parked out front.

Sammy pointed to the office at the side of the building and said, 'Just go in there and ask for Ken, the personnel manager.'

I wandered into this dark, musty, dingy office lined with old woodgrain panels. It looked a bit like a doctor's waiting room except it was full of big, hairy miners, all sitting round filling out job application forms.

In those days, all you had to do was peel off an application form from a pad on the counter, then fill it out, hand it to the office lady and walk out. If there was a job going, they might call you – or they might not. It was the luck of the draw.

To get a start in the industry back then, you needed to have a police clearance, a miner's health surveillance card, which lasted five years, and a truck licence. There were no drug tests, medicals, inductions, relevant machine tickets, logbooks and various other courses you need to have nowadays. But once you got a foot in the door and had the personnel manager's phone number, you were away laughing. A quick call on the phone and you could just walk in there, bypass all the big, hairy miners filling out application forms, poke your head around the personnel manager's door, sit down in his office and he would reel off all the sites that needed operators or dump truck drivers.

I approached the front counter. The elderly receptionist looked up at me, over her glasses.

'Hello, love, what can I do for you?' she asked.

'I'm here to see Ken,' I said, then gave her my name.

'Oh, okay, just take a seat, darl, and fill this out,' she said, handing me an application form. 'He'll see you shortly.'

I sat down with all the big, hairy miners. A guy with three days' growth on his face looked at me. 'How ya going, bloke?' he asked.

'Yeah, good,' I replied.

'They say Kanny's has a permanent bus at the airport to shuttle blokes straight to this office,' he told me.

Just as I was about to reply, a man popped his head around the door and called out: 'Mike Bellamy?'

The big, hairy miner piped up, 'How come you can just jump the queue, bloke?'

'You should have jumped on the same Kanny's bus as me, mate!' I grinned at him and walked casually into Ken's office.

'Right, Mike, what experience do you have?' Ken asked.

'Oh, about four or five years on excavators and dozers.'

'Okay, that's good. What size and sorts of jobs have you done?'

'One-and-a-half to 40-tonne excavators, digging footings and house sites.'

'Hmm … What about dozer work?'

'Umm, I've driven a D7 logging, an International TD-15 and a Komatsu D21A dozer doing floor preps and car parks.'

It was clear that Ken was trying not to laugh. 'Do you realise our diggers are 65 to 180 tonnes?'

I should have bullshitted like everyone else, but I was only 21 and a bit green.

Ken wrote some things down, then shook my hand. He said he would get back to me and asked for a contact phone number, so I gave him the hotel's number as there were no mobile phones back then.

Outside Sammy asked what site they were sending me to.

'I don't know, Sam, he didn't offer me a job.'

'What? You must be joking! They're screaming out for blokes and you've come all this way …'

I was a bit gutted.

The next day, Sam and Dino and I decided to head out to the casino at Burswood, which was a bit of a novelty for me. Before we left, I'd let the hotel reception know where I would be, just in case Ken rang.

At about six o'clock, I was called to reception at the casino to take a phone call. By then, I was full as a boot.

'Gidday,' I answered, trying not to slur.

'It sounds like you're having a good time,' said the voice on the other end of the line. It was Ken. 'Listen, could you be at our yard tomorrow morning? A chap called Mark will give you a lift up to Eon's gold mine at Wiluna. I'm going to put you on one of our production diggers.'

I told Ken that would be fine and hung up before wandering back to find Sammy.

'Hey, I've got a start,' I told him.

'Cool! You coming with us to Mount Gibson then?'

'Nah, a place called Wiluna.'

'Wiluna!' cried Sammy. 'You were supposed to be coming with us …'

I was a bit disappointed not to be going with Sam, but I was happy to have a foot in the door to the mining industry.

That night, we decided to spend just $20 each at the casino and anyone who got too carried away would have his wallet taken off him. We were all having a good time when Dino staggered off into the crowd and disappeared.

After about an hour, Sam started to get a bit worried about him. He needn't have, though, as Dino soon came staggering back towards us with a big grin on his face.

'Have a look at this,' he said, holding out his hand, which was full of casino chips.

Apparently, he'd placed a bet on the table then forgotten about it. As he'd wandered off, he heard a woman calling out after him, so he returned to the table.

'Sorry, love, did I do something wrong?' he asked.

Apparently, she'd looked at him, very confused and said, 'No, sir, you just won $900.'

The drinks – and a meal and a taxi back to the hotel – were on Dino!

2

London, Paris, Wiluna

I TOOK A TAXI out to Welshpool to meet up with Mark. When I got there, I found him leaning on an old, white Valiant car.

I introduced myself and we had a bit of a chat before deciding to hit the road. Once in the car, I asked Mark how far it was to Wiluna as I had no idea where it was.

'Ah about ten-and-a-half hour's drive, and a bit over 900 k's or thereabouts,' he replied casually, as if it was just up the road.

I thought, man, this is a big country.

'What are you doing at Wiluna? I asked.

'On a dumpie. What about you, mate?'

'Oh, a digger,' I answered. 'First time in the mines.'

'Don't worry, Mick. The novelty will soon wear off,' he said with a grin.

As we headed out of Perth, the scenery rolled by. After about four hours, the trees began to get smaller and smaller and the highway got narrower and straighter, to the point where it was just a bitumen strip a truck-width wide with a red gravel strip on either side.

We drove on the narrow bitumen strip until a car approached from the opposite direction, at which point, Mark would quietly steer half the car over onto the gravel, leaving the other half on the bitumen. He did this manoeuvre all while carrying on at 110 kilometres an hour (and the rest). The other cars did the same.

If a road train approached from the opposite direction, Mark would slow down and pull right off the bitumen strip to give the road train right of way and avoid getting a smashed window from one of the 62-plus tyres as they thundered past. If a road train was to swing onto the gravel, all the bull dust it kicked up would leave us with zero visibility.

Despite the risk they posed, I was excited to see all the road trains passing by with their two or three long trailers.

Mark carried on driving kilometre after kilometre and the further we went, the hotter it got and the old Valiant had no air-con. The trees had been replaced by spinifex and scrub, and the landscape was almost flat as far as the eye could see. The road in front of us stretched straight to the horizon. To me, the scenery looked like a last frontier, untouched by man – until, that is, I saw an old gold mine waste dump sticking out like a sore thumb in the distance.

My daydreaming was interrupted when Mark piped up: 'Hey, Mick, I hope Ken didn't tell you any porkies. All those personnel guys are the same, you know. They lie through the skin of their teeth and promise you the world – tell you the dirt boss is a saint, the gear's all new and the camp is five star ... Then you bloody get on site to find the boss is a screaming skull, your dump truck is a rattle crate with over 20,000 hours on the clock and your donga leaks like a sieve.'

After driving for about five hours, we stopped at Paynes Find for a bite to eat, some fuel and a chance to stack up the Esky with tinnies or, as Mark put it: 'A couple of roadies for on the way.'

Back on the road, he cracked opened a tinnie and took a big swig before belching and wiping his mouth with the back of his hand.

'Yep, she's a good drop, the old Emu Export, ain't she?' he said, sticking the tinnie between his legs so he could fish around in the glovebox for his old, battered, greasy stubbie holder, which he then slipped over his cold beer.

As the kilometres rolled by, Mark piped up again: 'We're nearly at Meeka, Mick, so we'll stop for a cold one at the Royal Mail Hotel, which I heard is a good pub. How's that sound?'

It sounded good to me. I was melting and it was 40-plus degrees outside, so I was looking forward to sitting in an air-conditioned pub.

Meekatharra was a small town where everything was stained red by bull dust. Given its size, it had a surprising number of pubs.

We pulled up outside the Royal Mail Hotel, slowly climbed out and had a big stretch. Gathered under the verandah of the old pub was a group of locals in their red-stained jeans. Despite the heat, they were all standing on the footpath in bare feet, which didn't seem to faze them.

I stepped over two skinny, mangy-looking dogs having a snooze on the footpath.

'Crikey, Mark, this place is like the Wild West – it's so remote,' I said.

He laughed. 'Wait till you see Wiluna …'

Inside the pub, I pulled up a stool at the bar while Mark went off to talk to a couple of the locals.

'What'll it be, love?' the barmaid asked.

'Oh, I'll have a glass of that Swan Lager, thanks,' I replied, pointing to the Swan logo on the tap.

'Okay, one midi of super coming up, darl,' she said.

When Mark came over, he was fuming. 'I was just talking to that old prospector over there. He reckons that the road from here to Wiluna isn't sealed! What did I tell you, mate? What did I tell you? They never tell the truth. Well, stuff Ken if he thinks he's pulling a shonky and taking a lend of me. I'll get on the blower and sort it out,' he shouted, as he stormed off to phone the office back in Perth.

Ten minutes later, he wandered back in looking pleased with himself. 'Sorted that slippery bugger out, Mick,' he said.

'They're sending a Land Cruiser from Wiluna to escort us – be here in about two-and-a-half hours.'

'Rightio,' I replied, 'I may as well have another midi of super then.'

Three-and-a-half hours and many midis of super later, we heard the engine brake of a road train as it pulled up outside the pub.

I glanced over the batwing doors and noticed a bloke climbing out of the passenger side of the cab, looking a bit worse for wear. When he walked into the bar, I noticed the logo on his shirt – Kanny's. He was clearly looking for us.

Milton introduced himself. 'Look, sorry I'm late but the Land Cruiser broke down so they're sending a fitter out from our Gabanintha mine site about 40 k down the road to tow it back,' he explained. 'He'll pick us up on the way back through, so we'll all camp at Gabanintha tonight and head out tomorrow morning.'

We managed to catch the dining room at the mine camp just before it closed. A good meal helped us both sober up before we went to sleep.

The next morning, Mark left early to beat the heat of the day, but he decided I'd be better off in the air-conditioned Land Cruiser, so I waited and got a lift with Milton.

As we drove the 45 kilometres back to Meekatharra, the horizon lit up fiery red, casting its light and shadows on the red, rocky ground. Nothing beats a desert sunrise, I thought.

Heading out of Meekatharra towards Wiluna, Milton turned right onto a red gravel road. Out in the middle of nowhere, standing on the side of the road, was a local, waiting to hitch a lift. He wasn't even carrying a backpack or anything.

Milton pulled over and called out, 'Hey, Billy, how you been?' You want a ride, bloke?'

'Yeah, mate, good on ya! I'll just jump on the back,' Billy replied.

I turned to Milton and said, 'There's plenty of room in the front.'

'You don't mind, Mick?' Milton asked.

I thought it was bit strange that he'd even ask. 'Of course I don't,' I replied.

With the nod from Milton, Billy climbed into the cab as I shuffled over, into the middle of the bench seat. He was dressed in red-dust-stained jeans, a red-dust-stained checked shirt and cowboy boots. Out there, it was impossible to keep red dust off your clothes.

'Just came down from up north. Big get-together with the mob,' Billy said.

'How long you up there, Billy?' Milton asked.

'Oh, about a week.'

Milton dropped the clutch on the old Land Cruiser, and off we went, bouncing and rattling our way down the highway.

Sitting on the edge of the Western Desert, the township of Wiluna had a population of about 600 people, but many more worked in the nearby mines. It's at the southern end of the Canning Stock Route, which runs 1850 kilometres north east to Halls Creek in the Kimberley region. About 350 kilometres to the east of Wiluna is the Gunbarrel Highway, an isolated track which connects Western Australia, the Northern Territory and South Australia. The track was built by Len Beadell – whose books I was a big fan of – back in the 1950s as part of the infrastructure to allow the testing of nuclear weapons in the Australian hinterland.

After 180 kilometres, we pulled up outside the pub in Wiluna. Billy hopped out of the truck and thanked Milton for the ride.

'No worries, Billy,' Milton replied before turning to me and saying, 'Hey, Mick, I'm just popping into the pub to get some smokes. Won't be a tick.'

I waited in the truck with the window down. The first thing I noticed was the flies, millions of them. Little buggers. They love any spot that's damp, and I soon found them heading for the corners of my eyes. My sunglasses didn't deter them. The little sods just buzzed around between my eyes and the lenses, driving me nuts. They flew up my nose and down my throat. I soon learned that if I was engaged in a deep and meaningful conversation with a mate and he started gagging, hocking, spitting, I shouldn't be offended – he was still listening, it was just likely he'd swallowed a fly!

The heat and flies finally got to me, so I bailed out of the old Land Cruiser and shot into the pub.

Milton spotted me and finished talking to a station hand, who was his cousin. He wandered over, apologising for having left me outside for so long. Together, we walked back to the Land Cruiser.

You can spot a mine from miles away. There's always either a waste dump with its benched layers of rock sticking out of the flat landscape like a mini-mountain, or – if it's an underground mine – a headframe. These headframes look like giant steel towers that are braced diagonally on one side. Up top they have huge pulley wheels, which work on the same principle as an elevator. They run on wire cables to winch the ore out of the mine.

Soon, we pulled up at the Eon mine camp. For its time, the camp was quite flash with its neat rows of dongas – temporary, transportable cabins providing accommodation – with their awnings jutting out to provide much-needed shade, green lawns – well, patchy, green lawns – in stark contrast to the harsh, red, rocky landscape with spinifex and scrub as far as the eye could see. There was even a swimming pool!

Most mine camps were run by private contractors and we lived under their rules not the rules of the company that employed us. While staying in camp, if you were a naughty boy and played up, the contractor could ban you from their accommodation – and there was nowhere else in the outback to stay, so it would be onto the next flight home for you.

This big, fat bloke, who was dressed as a chef, walked over to me and introduced himself as Bert, the camp manager and cook.

As we shook hands, he said, 'I will tell you now, lad, my golden rules: no parties after ten o'clock and no letting off fire extinguishers around the camp. No smoking in the dongas – or any funny stuff, for that matter.'

'Okay, yeah, got that,' I replied.

Bert was huge, and I mean round, not tall. He was shaped like a barrel in that his backside stuck out just as much as his stomach. I nicknamed him Big Bert – not to his face, of course, otherwise I'd probably have got a frying pan around my earhole.

Bert showed me the way to my donga. As he opened the door, the smell of old lino wafted up into my nostrils. The room had a single bed, a writing desk with a white plastic chair, and a little beer fridge in a corner.

On one wall was a door that opened into the bathroom, which had a toilet and a shower. These were shared, so another door on the other side of the bathroom opened into my next-door neighbour's donga. As it turned out, my neighbour was Milton, which was good as we got on well. Milton was a blast-hole drill-rig operator but I found out later that he didn't do much drilling because the mining company we were working for didn't want to pay for it.

When we met up again outside, Milton said, 'Chuck your boots on, Mick, and I'll take you over to the mine site to meet Ivan, the dirt boss.'

I was all excited as we pulled up outside the mine office. I could see the dump trucks going back and forth, up and onto the waste dump, before tipping off in a cloud of dust. I also watched the old Mack water cart spraying the haul roads. There was an old Caterpillar 16G grader removing some spillage from a bend in the haul road. Any spillage on a haul road can slice dump-truck tyres like a razor blade.

Meanwhile, a CAT D9L dozer was pushing off the rock, over the edge of the waste dump. I could hear its reversing alarm beeping away and the clatter of its tracks going back and forth. I'd only ever seen this sort of gear in the pages of mining magazines, so I thought it was hot stuff to see it all actually working.

My thoughts were broken when this gorilla of a man walked up to me.

'You Mick?' he asked.

'Yes, that's me,' I replied as I reached my hand out to shake his. His name was Ivan and he nearly broke my hand.

'Good. You come with me. I run you out to da pit,' he said. 'We got three pits: M1, M2 and M3. You be in M1 for a while. We got water problems. Big pain in butt.'

At least, I think that is what he said. He had a strong Slavic accent and I could only understand about every third word.

Ivan ran me down to the digger in his Land Cruiser. The M1 pit looked huge to me and quite deep. Down at the bottom of it was a near-new, 70-tonne CAT 245 BME excavator which was loading 50-tonne 773B dump trucks. The gear also looked huge to me.

Ivan pulled up beside the digger and the leading hand, Brent, climbed out of its cab. He was a solid bloke sporting a three-day growth and a nasty scowl on his face. He took one look at me, smirked, then jumped in with Ivan. No handshake, nothing.

As I climbed up into the digger, I was a bunch of nerves. It was the biggest digger I had seen at the time. There were no company or site inductions in those days – just throw on your work clobber and get digging.

I revved the digger and started digging, not really knowing what to do. I had a rough idea and I did my best to remember what Sammy had told me. He had been right – it wasn't rocket science.

In a gold mine, they drill the pit floor five metres deep and blast it. Once blasted, the digger or bulldozer will cut a ramp in, roughly two-and-a-half metres deep. This is called a drop cut and the dump trucks use it to back down to the bottom of the pit and that becomes the new RL (floor) level. The digger stays on the level above the dump truck, which becomes his bench, and digs out strips across the pit two-and-a-half metres deep, taking the ore and waste out as he goes. After that, he'll come back and put in another drop cut and sit on that bench and dig the last two-and-a-half metres down to solid rock, which is the toe.

Then the procedure starts all over again until they have worked their way down 20 metres. They'll leave five metres of the floor beside the pit wall, which becomes the berm. Next, they'll drill and blast another 20 metres at five-metre intervals to whatever depth the pit is designed to be. And that's how mine pits get that terraced look.

At Eon, M1 was the only pit that was drilled and blasted. The other two shallower pits were free digging pits. These were still a nightmare to dig as the clay was tight and most of the time I needed a dozer to rip it for me.

Meanwhile, the dump trucks would queue up. We ran three 50-tonne 773s below the digger.

In the digger, I would chip and scrape and get knocked around like a rag doll for 12 hours a day, sometimes breaking the adaptors that held the rock tooth onto the bucket. No wonder they went through so many digger drivers.

Bob, the fitter, joked about the hall of fame up on the wall of their workshop. It was a list, written in black marker pen, of all the digger drivers who had come and gone. The fitters had to work out in a harsh environment, in an open tin shed for a workshop, in temperatures of 40 to 45 degrees for 12 hours, including trying to fix red-hot machines that had just broken down.

There was no one week on and one week off, or two weeks on and one week off in those days. It was six to eight weeks on and one week off for us.

3

Caterpillar can opener

I WAS DOWN IN the bottom of M1 pit one day. It was nearly the end of the shift. Sometimes I would have to stay back and pull the batters (trim the slope). I was struggling to pull the batter. I was chipping, banging and scraping, trying my best, while also trying my patience, when there was a crackle on the radio. It was Ivan. He was parked at the lookout on top of the pit, peering down on me.

'What are you bloody playing at, Mick? Dig the bloody thing. Stop mucking around with dat machine,' he yelled over the radio.

Then Brent piped up with his two cents' worth: 'Stop being a fluff and give it shit!'

I muttered to myself, 'Pair of tossers. They'll keep.' If I had answered back, I would probably have been sacked.

The problem with mining in those days was that if you weren't covered in tattoos and didn't have a goatee or a three-day growth to make yourself look tough, you didn't exactly fit in. Some bosses made a sport out of picking on blokes. It was best to just let it go in one ear and out the other if you wanted to keep your job.

It was the start of the wet season. Heavy rain had washed all the sheeting off the haul road down onto the bottom of the pit floor. Sheeting is a layer of gravelly material that covers the haul road so that it doesn't cut the tyres on the dump trucks. It gives the grader something to trim off and makes the haul road smooth riding for the dump trucks.

I was sitting on my bench watching Brent, who was on the D9L dozer. He was trying to push all the slop from the sheeting material up to my digger so I could load it out and onto the dump trucks. He was putting on a big act, screaming around all over the pit floor with the dozer in third gear – something you should never do.

Over to one side was a deep sump hole blasted out of solid rock. The groundwater would be pumped out of the sump hole to make sure the bench level above stayed as dry as possible in a 60-metre-deep pit.

Anyway, Brent was flying around, showing us how good he was and how it was done in the slop. He started to work his way over to where the sump hole was, but as it was filled with sloppy mud, he couldn't see it.

'Hey, Brent, remember there's a sump hole there somewhere, mate,' I called over the radio.

'Course I bloody know,' he replied.

What he didn't know was that we'd blasted a new sump hole when he was away on his week off.

Next minute, his dozer disappeared into the sump hole and then there was silence.

'Are you all right, Brent?' I asked, trying hard not to laugh.

The radio crackled. 'You find that funny?' demanded a furious Brent.

'Oh well, mate, look on the bright side. At least your radio hasn't drowned,' I replied.

Well, it all turned into a major. Ivan was away on his week-long break, so Dirk, a South African, was our relief dirt boss. He was a trouble shooter who was quite high up in Kanny's management. He also had a reputation for being sack-happy and it would be nothing for him to sack a whole crew back then.

I had to stop my dump trucks and Jacko, the other D9L dozer driver, had to park his scrapers up so we could go down into the pit to try and tow Brent out.

My first priority was to try to lower the water level in the sump hole around the dozer. The motor on a high-track dozer sits quite low in the machine, so this wasn't easy. While the dozer looks high, under the bonnet most of it is cosmetic, with the space filled up with mufflers and an air cleaner.

Before long, Bob, the fitter, came rattling down the haul road in his old Land Cruiser, towing a huge, thick wire tow rope.

He hopped out, took one look and said, 'Hmm, you blokes have got yourselves into a bit of a pickle, haven't you?' Then he started taking the mickey: 'Any of you boys got a rowboat so I can row over to the dozer and cut her fan belt? I can't swim! Who's the drongo who drowned it? Must be you, Brent, you're all covered in crap. Look, here's a knife – there's no point two of us getting covered in slop, so away you go, bloke, and cut that belt. Uncle Dirk over there's got a face like thunder. Looks like he's going to sack someone shortly.' Bob seemed to think it was hilarious.

Jacko backed up the other D9L dozer, put his ripper boot through the eye of the tow rope, then did the same on Brent's dozer. Jacko took the strain on the rope, then pulled up with the ripper to try to drag Brent's dozer up the solid rock wall of the sump. It didn't work. The wet ground meant he was slipping and sliding and wasn't able to get any traction.

By this time, Brent's dozer was starting to cook. If they didn't cut the fan belt soon, the fan blades would explode in the water and go through the radiator.

Dirk walked up and shouted, 'If dis dozer is not out by three o'clock, you're all sacked!' Then he stormed off.

Bob winked at me. 'Don't worry, Mick. He'll get a spanner round his left listener in a minute if he carries on with that caper. Jump on your digger and put your rock tooth through that eye on the tow rope with Jacko's ripper. Together, you should be able to skull drag her out of that sump, mate.'

I did what Bob told me and it worked. After a bit of yanking and pulling, we finally got the 50-odd-tonne dozer out of the sump hole, but unfortunately its motor was cooked. Bob reckoned it'd cost about $100,000 for a new motor.

Dirk couldn't sack Brent. Brent didn't know about the new sump hole and it wasn't in his nature to thank anyone.

* * *

Jacko was a short, thin, young bloke, around 25 years old, with a mop of blond hair. He always had his shirt off. He was in charge of push-loading two 651E scrapers, driven by Ben and Nick. They'd been tasked with moving an old waste dump and digging a new key way for a tailings dam wall. Ben was in his late twenties and sported a long, brown mullet. Nick was a big, burly olive-skinned bloke, with straight black hair. He was about Brent's size, a nice guy and a real larrikin. Unfortunately, Brent had taken an almost immediate dislike to Nick and took every opportunity to try to get him sacked.

I was digging in M2 pit one day and hit a hard spot that I couldn't dig, and the trucks started to queue up. Nick was on a dump truck that day, so he was parked up, waiting to back under my bucket while I was scraping and chipping, trying to catch up. Kanny's had hired a new dump truck driver, Dazza, who wasn't popular. As Brent put it, Dazza was a real mung bean.

Dazza pulled up in the queue and tried to park his dump truck beside Nick but misjudged and clipped the front corner of Nick's dump truck. Brent heard about it on the radio and came screaming down in his old, beaten up dual-cab ute.

'You're both sacked,' he gleefully yelled on the radio.

I piped up on and asked, 'How can you sack Nick when he's parked up, minding his own business?'

There was silence for a second.

'So, you saw it happen then, Mick?' Brent asked.

'Sure did.'

'Oh, so it was Dazza's fault then?'

'Yep,' I replied.

I think Brent was a bit disappointed that it wasn't Nick's fault, but down the road Dazza went.

After that, Nick and I became friends, but Brent still wasn't done with him.

One night, they were both drinking in the wet mess when Brent baited Nick, trying to get him to arm wrestle. It turned out that Brent had heard that Nick had broken his wrist and he'd only had his cast taken off a few weeks beforehand.

'Come on, Nick, are you man or mouse? Or are you just a blow arse?' Brent challenged him.

Nick just glared at him, knowing if he accepted the challenge, it would probably break his wrist again. But he'd had one too many beers and enough of Brent's taunting, so he said, 'Come on then, let's do it!

Everyone gathered around the table. Both men were the same stocky build, so it was an even match.

Brent and Nick locked hands.

Someone counted, 'Three! Two! One!' and they were away.

Before anyone could blink, Nick slammed Brent's hand down on the table then quietly looked at him and murmured, 'We can take it outside and finish it once and for all, you blow arse.'

Brent had finally met his match.

* * *

We were rained off in the pit one day, but Nick and Ben carried on moving an old waste dump out of the way with their 651E motor scrapers, with Jacko push loading them on his D9L dozer.

Somehow, Nick managed to talk our new leading hand, Tom, into letting me have a go on the scraper. I had a play on it, dug some holes, made a mess then left them to it. Getting to have a play on one of the largest scrapers Caterpillar made was a real buzz.

The following morning, when I got to work, I found Kanny's float driver, Albert, backing a third 651E scraper off the back of his float trailer. He was an old bloke with a face as corrugated as a bush track and he'd been driving for years. His old Kenworth truck was not only his home, but it was also his pride and joy.

The scraper needed to have a new radio fitted, so Albert drove it into Bob's workshop nose first, leaving its rear end sticking out. He then hobbled over to his Kenworth and parked his big float trailer out of the way, before uncoupling the float trailer and parking his tractor unit in the middle of the yard, out of harm's way.

That evening it poured down, so the next morning we were all rained off again. The weather had been so bad that the road had been closed because of flooding. Road trains chew up gravel roads in the wet season, so the Shire was quick to close the roads to stop this from happening. It also issued big fines to anyone caught in a truck on a closed road. As a result of all this, the road train diesel tanker couldn't get through and we'd run out of diesel in the main storage tanks on the mine site.

Outside, it was still drizzling. It had rained on the Wednesday for a couple of hours in the evening, and the water was still flowing over the main road on the Sunday. The water was slowly making its way out from deep in the outback desert.

We were all sitting in the smoko shed playing cards or reading well-thumbed *Picture* magazines when Bob poked his head round the door. 'Sorry to wake you blokes, but can one of you misfits move that bloody scraper out of my workshop so I can have some space?'

A dump truck driver nicknamed Agro jumped up straight away and yelled, 'I'll do it!'

'Didn't know you could drive a scraper, Agro?' I said.

'Course I can, Mick. Nothing to it,' he replied, and darted out of the smoko hut.

A bit later, we heard the V12 scraper motor fire up, then Agro revving the guts out of it.

As I was looking out the window into the yard, Agro revved the scraper once more before lifting the scraper bowl up, throwing the transmission into reverse and screaming backwards out of the workshop, flat out. He passed the smoko room window with a roar.

It was then I noticed all 65-and-a-half tonne of his scraper reversing towards old Albert's Kenworth tractor unit. Then I saw Albert's tractor unit moving along beside the scraper.

'Oh, shit!' I yelled as I charged off out the door and ran towards Agro.

He saw me flapping my arms like crazy and stopped.

'Crikey, Agro. Have a look around the other side, mate. It's not a pretty sight.'

He climbed down out of the cab and joined me.

'Oh, shit!' His face dropped. 'I'm sacked,' he said, as he looked at the side of old Albert's Kenworth buried into the draft arm of the scraper bowl. The passenger's side of his truck had been peeled away, leaving a gaping hole.

Later on, Albert was in the cab of his mangled Kenworth, getting his belongings out of the truck before it set off on its long trip back to Perth on the back of his float trailer.

I peered into his cab and watched him lovingly take his possessions out and I thought I'd cheer him up a bit. 'Hey, Albert! You've got to look on the bright side, mate. At least you've got really good vision out the passenger side when you're backing. And think of all the ventilation you'll have on those hot, balmy days cruising down the Great Northern Highway!'

'It's not bloody funny, Mick,' he said.

'Sorry, mate ... so when's the funeral?'

'You'll get a twitch thrown at you in a minute.'

'Sorry ... sorry ... I'll let you mourn in peace,' I said, then I ducked off to the smoko room before he blew a fuse.

* * *

Even though it was the wet season, it was still stinking hot. With no fuel getting into the site and the road still closed, we had come to a grinding halt. Nick was sitting in the smoko room with everyone else, waiting for the diesel to arrive.

It was a steamy 40-degree day. You can smell the outback after it rains. Everything comes alive. It even greens up for about two weeks before being burnt off again by the harsh sun.

'This is choice, eh, Nick? No work. Let's go walkabout and have a look around the mine site,' I suggested.

'Yeah, why not?' he replied. 'I was talking to one of Eon's blokes and he reckons you can swim in one of the ponds between M2 and M3 pits.'

'What, you fellas going for a swim?' Foxie piped up. He was one of the dumpie drivers – a funny bloke who always wore a battered old Akubra hat. 'Can I tag along?'

'Course you can,' I said.

Nick was the only one of us who had worked out near M3 pit. We packed our survival kit for the journey – half a dozen tinnies of Emu Export each in our backpacks – and not one of us gave a thought about carrying some water, just in case.

Off we wandered, sipping quietly on our first tinnie for the day. It was still morning, so it wasn't too hot, but, man, it was humid.

We followed a dirt track around the edge of the mine lease and a swarm of flies followed us as we went.

Ahead of us, to the horizon, was a vast wilderness of bush which had its own rugged beauty. Behind us was the mine site, and all we could see were piles of rock bulldozed up, piles of red topsoil stockpiled, big, rocky waste dumps towering over the site, water pumps and black poly-pipe snaking all over the site for dewatering of the pits, 44-gallon drums lying around, old mining dump-truck tyres painted white and used as roundabouts, four-wheel drive tyres filled with concrete to hold up 'Stop' signs, ponds and sump holes dug everywhere, dirt tracks and haul roads criss-crossing the place and light-green ore-sample bags stacked in rows, or empty ones blowing all over the show – yeah, it wasn't the most attractive place to work.

After another two or three beers, which had heated up and tasted pretty awful, we finally strolled up to a row of ponds.

'Righto, Nick. Which pond is it? They all look the colour of tea,' I said.

'Blowed if I know,' said Nick. 'The Eon bloke just pointed over this direction …'

'Well, that one looks cleaner than the others,' Foxie said, pointing to one of the ponds.

I looked at the ponds. I'd heard they used all sorts of toxic chemicals in mine-site ponds. Cyanide for separating gold sprang to mind.

'Well, Nick,' I said, 'Since this was your brainwave of an idea, you can jump in first, mate, and see if it turns your toes up.'

Nick was standing there with his beer pot hanging over his jocks, scratching his backside as he finished off his tinnie. 'What a pair of fluffs,' he said, before doing a big bombie into the pond.

Foxie soon joined him. 'What are you waiting for, Mick?'

'Just waiting to see if you two mugs start dissolving,' I replied, as I gingerly dipped my big toe in the water.

A couple of weeks after that lucky dip, I was flying back to site in a little twin-engine plane after my week off. I hadn't flown much in those days, so I found it really interesting to gaze out the window at the vast red landscape below. The only problem with flying in such a little plane was that it bounced all over the show, and I started to feel sick. Fortunately, I soon spotted the mine's airstrip, which was a graded gravel strip right through the middle of a patch of scrub beside the mine site.

As we came in to land, the plane was nearly sideways in the wind. It's amazing what angle you can bring a plane in to land. We let out a collective sigh of relief as the plane touched down.

As the pilot opened the door, the flies and the searing heat were there to meet us, as was the camp boss, Big Bert.

'Hi, Bert. How's life treating you, mate?' I asked.

'Gidday, Mick. I've got something to show you back at camp,' he said in a serious tone.

'Oh, yeah? A new menu maybe?'

He glared at me. 'Bugger off, lad. You know what it is.'

I didn't know what it was.

As we pulled up back at camp, Bert pointed towards my donga and said, 'Right, come over here and look at this.'

We walked over to Milton's donga, next door to mine. Milton had snatched it and gone walkabout because there was not enough drill work.

'Right,' Big Bert yelled. 'Just look at that front door. Look at it!'

'Yeah, I'm looking, Bert. It's a door, all right,' I said, as I peered at it.

'How can you be so selfish, Mick? You just wanted the shower and toilet all to yourself. Is that why you did it?'

I had no idea what he was going on about, but it had something to do with Milton's door. I wriggled the door handle. It was locked.

'Ah, I see, Bert. You think I locked the door and pinched Milton's key?'

'Look down the doorframe, Mick.'

'Doorframe, doorframe – oh, I see! What a work of art!' I said, and dissolved into hysterics.

Someone had neatly drilled and pot-riveted about 10 rivets down the doorframe into the door.

I turned to Bert, my arms out in a wide gesture. 'Look, you got me, mate. Caught me red handed, no two ways about it.'

'Ah, so it was you!' He pointed one of his chubby little fingers at me accusingly.

'Yeah, course it was, Bert. I never leave home for the outback without first packing my power drill and a rivet gun in my suitcase. Never, ever,' I said, looking at him like he was a dimwit.

'Oh, so it wasn't you?' he asked, disappointed.

'Course it bloody wasn't,' I said.

Later on, I found out that Bert had sacked the caretaker, who, I would say, was the prime suspect.

4

If it doesn't bite, it stings you

GIVEN THE HARSH CLIMATE, it's amazing the wildlife that survives out in the bush. The place is teeming with life. On one of my days off, I was exploring out the back of camp, hunting for mineshafts and old bottles, when I looked up to find a red kangaroo sitting on its haunches, staring straight at me. I'm over six foot and I looked him in the eye – that's how tall he was. He hopped off one way and I ran off the other. I'd heard stories of them punching and kicking people and I didn't want to find out for myself if they were true.

I also saw the odd dingo skulking around the edge of camp. Bungarra lizards, which are also known as sand goannas, were everywhere. They're pretty harmless creatures but they can grow quite big – up to about six kilograms and over a metre long. Even though it wasn't allowed, the boys used to feed them and some of the bungarras got pretty brazen, coming into camp and occasionally tipping over rubbish bins.

I'd also spot the odd snake hiding under the donga. Like most camps, ours had a designated snake catcher – normally one of the blokes willing to take a crash course on how to catch a snake.

Seeing a snake for the first time, or any time for that matter, always gives you a fright. They appear when you least expect them and they are hard to spot, blending well into their surroundings. They are masters at hiding in little nooks and crannies, both indoors and outdoors. Some are tiny, but still deadly. Others, like pythons, are huge but relatively harmless.

While there's a bit of wildlife around in the daytime, it's at night that the Western Desert really comes alive. One night, while I was over in the wet mess having a coldie, I accidentally left the light on and my donga door open slightly.

When I came back and pushed open my door, the donga was black with wall-to-wall buzzing mosquitoes! The only way to deal with them was to cadge a can of fly spray off one of the boys. I emptied almost the whole contents of the can inside my donga before rushing out the door (closing it after me this time) and sneaking off for another tinnie in the wet mess.

The lighting around the camp wasn't the greatest, but thousands of big moths and beetles would come out at night and swarm around the light poles and, by morning, the ground around the poles would be covered in a mat of dead insects, some of them nine or ten centimetres long. There were some big, ugly creepy crawlies out there.

It was pretty common to be walking back from the wettie full as a boot and hear a crunch under the sole of your thongs, jandals, double-pluggers – whatever you want to call them.

One night, Nick walked into the wettie carrying a torch. He looked absolutely horrified.

'Blow walking around out in the dark anymore. Have you seen what's on the footpath out there, Mick?' he said.

'What? The boogie man?' I replied, and laughed.

'Grab my torch and have a look … you can find out for yourself,' he said, shaking his head.

I stepped out onto the dimly lit footpath, then turned on Nick's torch. The light of the torch revealed insects scuttling all over the footpath. I wondered what they were, as I'd never seen anything like them before. I peered down at one of them. It had a funny-looking curly tail with a nasty stinger on the end of it. Good grief! There were scorpions all over the place. So that's what had been crunching under my jandals as I walked home at night.

After one stinking hot 45-degree day, Nick, Foxie and I decided to take a few coldies and sit around the camp swimming pool. We threw our towels and clothes over the Super Six asbestos pool fence and jumped into the pool. Following a bit of clowning around and trying to drown each other, we all hopped out of the swimming pool, grabbed our towels and sat on them, leaning against the pool fence for a bit of shade.

A couple of beers later, I reached up for my tee shirt, which was draped over the pool fence. As I was pulling my tee shirt off the fence, I spotted the biggest redback spider I'd ever seen, sitting under the fence's ridge capping. On closer inspection, I saw that the ridge capping was teeming with redbacks right above Foxie's and Nick's heads. I quietly moved my towel away and sat out in the open.

'Hey, Foxie, do you like redback spiders?' I asked.

'Redbacks!' Foxie's voice boomed out. 'Redbacks! Don't mention redbacks to me. They give me the creeps.'

Then I asked Nick if he liked them.

'Nah, don't really like them either,' he replied.

'Oh, so if I said – hypothetically, of course – that there's a nest of them about two feet away from you two, what would you say?'

'I'd say you're losing your marbles, Mick,' said Nick as looked under his towel then nervously peered around and behind himself.

I cracked open another tinnie and stuffed it in my stubbie holder and asked, 'What's wrong with redbacks? They share their habitat with us, hiding away, minding their own business, living a life right under our noses ...'

'Sounds like you're going troppo, Mick, or watching too many nature docos,' Foxie snorted.

After another half hour of taking a lend of them, I decided I'd better tell Nick and Foxie the truth. 'If you two blokes really don't like redbacks, you'd better grab your clothes off the fence.'

They both looked up to the fence at the same time and their reactions were priceless.

'Aagh, ugh, look at them all! Thanks for bloody telling us!' cried Foxie.

'They're so creepy! They make my skin crawl. Disgusting!' said Nick, shaken. 'Enough to give a bloke nightmares ...'

They both vigorously shook out their clothes at arm's length, standing well away from the fence, like it was electric. From my vantage point out in the open, I found the whole spectacle quite entertaining.

But I reckon the creepiest insect encounter I had at Wiluna was the night when I dreamt something was scratching my face. The dream was so vivid that I woke up suddenly, to find something walking over my face. Straightaway I thought it was a spider and, in a panic, fumbled around for the light switch, hoping not to get bitten at the same time.

When I finally managed to switch the light on, right in front of my eyes, on the pillow beside me, I saw two long feelers flicking back and forth. They were attached to a five-centimetre-long bush cockroach, which was staring at me intently. It was ugly – and quick, as I found out, as I chased it around the donga trying to squash it, waking up my neighbour in the process.

One morning, not long after the drama of the redbacks, I cadged a ride down into the M1 pit with Foxie in his old, beaten-up 777B dump truck. Most dump trucks have a dickey seat for the passenger, either beside the driver or behind him. These dump trucks had been around the moon and back. They would always billow out black smoke just as they pulled away from the digger, ready to grind their way out of the pit and up to the waste dump.

Foxie and I climbed up the ladder into the cab of his 777B dump truck. I sat beside him while he fumbled for his pen, which was poked into the head lining of the roof.

'It's a piece of junk, eh, Mick?'

I peered around the inside of the red, dust-stained cab. 'Yep, she's seen better days,' I agreed.

As Foxie fired up the engine, the stale stink of the old air-con wafted through the cab.

Wearing his battered, old Akubra hat, Foxie was leaning over the steering wheel, filling out his pre-start and load sheet. The old 777 was quietly idling away. In their wisdom, Caterpillar had channelled the exhaust fumes out of the exhaust and up into the dump tray, then along the inside of the dump tray and out of a hole in the back of the dump tray, the reason being the heat of the fumes would warm the dump tray and stop the load sticking. But the poor old digger driver up on the bench would quietly get asphyxiated by the exhaust fumes. In those days, the CAT 245 diggers had a really short dipper arm for breakout power, and the digger driver struggled to reach to the front of the dump truck when loading, which meant that the back of the dump truck tray was just about in his face.

Foxie finally finished his paperwork and poked his pen back up into the head lining, then turned to me with a grin. The dump truck had been idling for at least 10 minutes.

'Hey, Mick, watch this: it's an oldie but a goodie,' he said. Then he put the dump truck in gear and quietly crept it forward about two or three feet, before muttering, 'That should do.'

I looked out the window and across at young Reg in the other 777B, which was parked right beside us. He had his door open and was filling out his paperwork. When he looked over at me, I gave him the fingers and he responded with an equally rude gesture while Foxie quietly lifted the tray of his dump truck up. The sound of his idling engine changed as the exhaust pipe was parted from the dump tray. This left a straight stub of the exhaust pipe sitting out the side, in line with young Reg's head.

Foxie called up Reg on the two-way radio: 'Copy, Reg?'

'Yeah, copy,' Reg replied.

'You might want to take a deep breath, mate,' said Foxie over the two-way. He floored the accelerator. Brrrmm, brrrmm, brrrmm, brrrmm, the engine screamed, as thick, black smoke billowed out from Foxie's exhaust and spewed into young Reg's cab, and young Reg's dump truck disappeared from sight, in a cloud of black smoke.

Suddenly Ivan's voice boomed out over the two-way: 'You two! Stop bloody clowning around and get down to da pit before I sack you.'

* * *

As well as unusual creatures, the mines were also full of interesting people. The mining companies hired people from all walks of life. I met a lot of ex-tradies, an ex-furniture polisher, a cabinetmaker, a butcher and even one guy I was told was an ex-conman. Don't ask me how you just stop being a conman, but – yeah – he'd turned over a new leaf, apparently.

There weren't many women working in the mines back then. There were only two female dumpie drivers on site, which wasn't surprising as a lot of dirt bosses were pretty sexist. I don't know why, because the women drivers had a lot going for them. They seemed to have a longer attention span and they didn't get bored during night shift and start doing donuts in their dump trucks up on the waste dump just after the water cart had gone by. They didn't short dump their loads and thrash the guts out of their dump trucks while trying to race their mate back into the pit. And their two-way radio etiquette was a hell of a lot better than the boys'. You wouldn't hear them having conversations like this one over the radio ...

'Hey, Jono?'

'Yeah, Gazza?'

'How many stubbies did you knock back at the wettie last night, mate?'

'About a dozen.'

'A dozen! You soft cock. I drank a carton. But, gees, I'm still a bit seedy. Feel like snatching it.'

Of course, there were a lot of personalities in the mix, but most of the blokes had a good sense of humour. You needed one, to be stuck out in the middle of nowhere, working and living together.

One of our dump truck drivers was Jacques, a little Frenchman who wore steel-rimmed glasses and looked just like your stereotypical onion seller at a French market. He also had a very strong French accent.

One night, I got woken by the sound of someone yelling in a mixture of French and English: 'Get out, get out, get out. Do you think I'm queer, monsieur? Well, I'm not queer!' came Jacques' voice, echoing down the row of dongas.

I jumped out of bed and poked my head out the door just in time to see Ben the scraper driver's lily-white bum as he sprinted down the row of dongas, followed by Jacques' red-dust-stained steel-capped boot.

Next morning, Ben and his car were gone.

'What was that all about last night, Jacques?' I asked him, while munching on a bit of toast at breakfast.

'Disgusting, Mick, absolutely disgusting,' he replied. 'I woke up to find Ben in my bed.'

'Maybe he was just drunk, mate, and staggered into the wrong donga by mistake. It happens.'

'Non, non, Mick. Let's just say he was pleased to see me, if you know what I mean,' said Jacques.

* * *

In the days before mobile phones, we didn't have too many options if we wanted to phone home. In fact, we only had one, depending on the remoteness of the mine site or how old the camp was. If you wanted to ring your lotus blossom, girlfriend, mistress, boyfriend or mate, standing out in the middle of the lawn, looking like the Tardis had just landed, was a phone booth. Nothing flash: just a phone in a booth with no door, in the middle of the desert. There might have been a door once, but I suspect it had been booted in years ago by some frustrated, hairy miner missing home.

Next to the booth was a long, narrow, wooden bench seat where a queue of homesick miners waited their turn to use the phone while shooing flies away and getting eaten alive by mosquitoes. In their wisdom, the bench builders had put the bloody thing right next to the phone booth, so this is what we would all hear as we sat on it waiting our turn:

Ring-ring, ring-ring, click. (The click was the phone card eating up $1 per minute.)

'Yeah, gidday, doll. How's it going?'

Click – there goes another minute.

'How are the kids? (pause) Really? She took her first steps?'

Click – there goes another minute.

Beep beep beep – the phone cuts off as the card runs out of credit.

'What a bloody rip-off!'

Slam.

The next bloke was rapt as he didn't have to wait any longer to use the phone.

Ring-ring, ring-ring, click.

'Hello, is that you, sweetheart? It's Daddy. Have you been a good girl? What have you been up to? Kiss, kiss, kiss. Put your little brother on.'

At this point, the chap beside me leaned over and, all beery breath, said, 'Gees, mate, I hope this bloke doesn't have too many kids or we'll be here all bloody night!'

Kids all having been spoken to, the next bloke gets his turn.

Ring-ring, ring-ring, click.

'Hi, it's Max. Max – you know – we met at the party? Oh, sorry, wrong number.'

Slam. Muttering.

Those ones made me laugh. But there were some blokes I really felt sorry for. They were the ones who really didn't want to be there. Their faces told their stories.

A family man missing his wife and kids would just sit there patiently, quietly waiting for his turn to make a call while everyone else around him was laughing and chatting away. His turn finally came around after an hour of waiting. His face lit up a bit as he slotted in his phone card.

Ring-ring, ring-ring, ring-ring, ring-ring. Click.

'Please leave your name and number after the beep.'

She'd gone out.

Newer camps had more phone booths dotted around them until, eventually, someone with a bit of nous decided to build proper phone booths inside the camp buildings. They were a bit more comfortable, but the call rates stayed the same – $1 a minute. It was a blatant rip-off by the phone company, which was raking it in off the back of workers who just wanted to be able to call home.

Talking of home, I'd been at Wiluna for a few swings, when I decided I'd done my dash.

When I did finally leave, Bert ran me to the airport and, just as I was stepping on to the plane, he said, 'Look, Mick, you're going now, so it doesn't matter, but did you really rivet the door shut?'

I laughed in reply and hopped on the plane, leaving him in suspense.

5

The outback is calling me

I LEFT WILUNA IN a bout of homesickness and headed back to New Zealand. After a month working for low wages in the pouring rain on an Auckland construction site, I'd had enough. I just couldn't stop thinking about the deep-blue desert sky of Western Australia. The remoteness of the place fascinated me. So, with $300 in my pocket, I jumped on a plane back to Perth.

When I got there, I rang Ken at Kanny's and he told me to head out to the office to see him about a job.

I took a taxi out to Welshpool and walked into Kanny's office. As usual, it was full of big, hairy miners filling out job application forms.

Like an old hand, I walked straight up to the desk. 'Hi, I'm here to see Ken,' I said.

Before the receptionist could speak, Ken's head popped around the door.

'Ah, Mick. I thought that was your voice. Come on in and take a seat!'

As I sat down at Ken's desk, I couldn't help noticing the huge pile of applications with little yellow stickers on them. On each of the stickers was written the bloke's name, the position and what site they were going to.

'You've got your work cut out for you,' I said, pointing to the pile.

Ken laughed. 'Sure have. We hire around 8,000 people a year,' he said. 'Bear in mind, we go 24 hours on most of our sites, and it includes fitters, servicemen, shot-firers – you name it – not just operators. Right, Mick, what site would you like to go to? I had Gabanintha in mind for you. How does that sound?'

'Hasn't that got asbestos down in the pit?' By this time, I'd spoken to a few of the boys who had done the rounds of the different Kanny's mine sites, so I had a rough idea of where to avoid.

'Yes, but you're given a mask and paper overalls to wear when working in that section of the pit.'

'I don't like the sound of asbestos, to be honest, Ken.' The boys had warned me that he'd offer me the crap sites first, just like he had with me and Wiluna.

'Okay,' he said, without batting an eyelid. 'What about Kurara mine site? It's about 80-odd k before Meeka. How does that sound?'

'It's not free digging, is it?' I asked suspiciously.

'No, no,' he replied. 'That site has a good budget and it's all drill and blast. Nice cream digging, Mick.'

I thought that sounded better than chipping and scraping all day, breaking the teeth off the bucket and stuffing my back up.

'Yep, sounds good, Ken.'

'Right, Mick. Give me a bell, say, five o'clock this afternoon and I'll give you your mobilisation-to-site details.'

'Yea, rightio, Ken. Cheers for that.'

All done and dusted, I thought, as I walked out of his office, past the big, hairy miners still trying to fill out their application forms and out into a nice, sunny, still winter's day with the sky an even deeper blue that I remembered.

At five o'clock that afternoon, I rang Ken.

'Ah yes, Mick. Be in the yard at four o'clock tomorrow morning for an early start. You can hop in with Albert, our float driver. He's taking some spare parts up to Kurara mine site.'

I had my marching orders.

As instructed, at four o'clock the following morning, I wandered into Kanny's yard, bleary-eyed, to see old Albert's Kenworth idling with its headlights on, waiting for me.

'Gidday, Albert, how you been, mate? Did they just buy you another old Kenworth to replace your other truck?' I asked.

He laughed. 'You know what Kanny's are like, Mick. They just bought me a second-hand cab off an old bloody road train and slapped it on, the tight arses.'

Soon, we headed off and Perth's city lights gradually faded away into the distance as we headed out onto the Great Northern Highway.

The view from the cab of a truck is great and it's hard to beat seeing the sun rise up over the outback, the fiery light slowly popping up above the horizon, bringing in a new day. Even Albert reckoned he never got sick of seeing the sunrise over the Western Desert in all the years he'd been trucking.

A few hours later, as we passed through Payne's Find, I thought my eyes were deceiving me. Instead of the red pindan spanning out for miles, the ground looked like it was covered with snow. On closer inspection, I realised it was, in fact, covered in snow-white wildflowers.

Albert piped up: 'Can't beat wildflower season, Mick. Twelve thousand varieties of wildflowers in WA, 60 per cent of them not found anywhere else in the world. That's a fact.'

By mid-afternoon, Albert and I turned off in the middle of nowhere and headed down a short gravel track into Kurara gold mine. The mine was quite well set up with its own crusher and gold-processing plant.

Albert pulled up outside Kanny's workshop, which, like most workshops up in the bush, looked like an open, corrugated-iron hay shed.

Pete, the leading hand, come out to meet me. He was an awesome old bloke, real laid back. 'Righto, Mick, I'll take you over to the camp and book you in,' he said once we'd introduced ourselves.

'What gear are you running on the mine site, Pete?' I asked.

He replied, 'Oh, we've got four CAT 777Bs and four Komatsu HD465 dumpies, two CAT dozers, an old D9H and a D9L, and a 16G grader. We've also got a couple of CAT 245 excavators and one Liebherr R 984 hundred-tonne digger.' At the time, that was the largest digger I had seen.

'Oh, and an old Mack R600 water cart,' he added.

We walked over to the camp, which was older than the Eon camp at Wiluna. My donga was in a row facing another row of dongas, with a concrete corridor down the middle and a tin roof between the two rows for shelter.

As I walked in, I noticed the dark, dingy, wood-grained panels on the walls. There was no TV in the room, but that wasn't unusual. Some blokes would take their own portable TVs to site with them. For the rest of us, if we wanted to watch TV, we went over to the TV room, where nine times out of ten, everyone would be sitting in a haze of smoke, watching the footy.

My donga had no toilet or shower, but it did have a single bed and a rattly old square-box air-conditioner on the wall.

So, yeah, first impressions of the camp were fairly depressing.

There were blocks of newer dongas further over, but most of the Kurara gold mine workers had those. As with most mining camps, as people left, you'd eventually work your way into a better donga.

After spending the night listening to the rattly old air-con and putting up with mozzies sneaking in through the gaps around it, I had breakfast over in the dining room before hopping onto our Toyota Coaster bus and heading out to the mine site.

Our dirt boss, Mackie, introduced himself. One look at him and straightaway I knew he wouldn't suffer fools. His crooked nose was a giveaway.

'Right, Mick, you're down in Central Pit, and you're lucky we only work day shift down there. It's got a moving high wall, which we're monitoring with our surveying equipment every morning. The other pit next door is Boomerang Pit, which goes around the clock. Our 984 Liebherr is down in that pit, and you're on our CAT 245 digger. It's a fairly late model, so don't wreck it. Right, let's get cracking. I'll run you down to the pit,' he said – no site induction required.

The Komatsu dumpies hauled out of Central Pit and the CAT 777s hauled out of Boomerang Pit. I was lucky Central Pit was fairly shallow and the digging was great. I also worked with a good bunch of dumpie drivers – Barney, Robbo and Richie.

At lunchtime, I caught up with the boys for a chat.

'Hey, Mick, watch Mackie, mate. He's a screamer and he'll pick on you for the smallest little reason,' warned Barney. Laughing, he added, 'Robbo's always stuffing up, so he cops it as well.'

'Bugger off! He yells at you two clowns as well,' Robbo protested.

They were right, though. Mackie seemed to pick on one person at random each day. Early one bright, sunny morning, I started to dig at the face of the bench, but it came up rock solid. After taking two bites with the digger, the bucket was chipping and scraping. I had hit a bit of rock that hadn't been blasted properly.

Immediately, on the two-way, I heard Mackie's voice: 'Bellamy, what are you fluffing around at? Make that thing dig!'

Before I could even argue my case, Mackie's Land Cruiser came speeding down the ramp into the pit. He jumped out and started heading my way.

Barney's voice piped up on the two-way radio: 'Look out, Mick. Mack attack. Mack attack at three o'clock.'

Richie was laughing. 'It's your turn today, Mick. You're in the poop now, mate.'

Robbo put his two cent's worth in. 'At least I know it's not me today! Put your earplugs in, Mick, and take one for the boys.'

'Good one, boys. Thanks for the encouragement,' I said just as Mackie opened my door. Over his shoulder, I could see the boys laughing and giving me the thumbs up from of their cab windows.

The stink of Bundy rum on Mackie's breath hit me and his eyes looked like crushed Jaffas, all bloodshot.

'Get out,' he slurred at me.

I stepped out onto the boardwalk that ran down the side of the excavator, and Mackie hopped into my seat.

'You've got to work that bloody bucket. Look! Like this,' he said.

I hung on for dear life as he tried to dig the bucket into the bench. He chipped and banged and scraped at the bench face, but to no avail.

Sheepishly, he climbed out of the cab. 'Bloody hard! Must be a bit of toe that hasn't been blasted properly,' he slurred.

Stuff this, I thought, as I looked into his bloodshot, bleary eyes. 'Look, mate,' I said, 'if I'm no bloody good, sack me or bugger off.'

Mackie grinned at me and said, 'I would have tramped you by now if I was going to, Mick,' then he climbed down off the digger and drove away.

* * *

There was a bit of friction between the Kurara staff and Kanny's boys. Kurara staff looked down us. They were given better dongas and were allowed to fly in and out of camp, whereas we were only allowed to fly out if a seat became available at short notice. Even then, at the mine airstrip, they could turn you away at the last minute and this happened quite a bit, so it was drive-in, drive-out for us – or take the Greyhound bus.

In his wisdom, Mackie decided to organise a nice social get-together, a friendly game of footy – Kanny's versus Kurara – to help mend the ties that had been broken and to bond us as one unit again. One problem, though – we didn't have a footy field.

Mackie turned to Ronnie, one of our grader drivers, who looked like one of the singers from ZZ Top.

'Righto, Ronnie, crank up the old grader, mate, and clear me about two or three acres of that crappy-looking scrub and spinifex over on that flat bit of ground by our old waste dump. Oh, plus make us a bit of a track through those mulga trees for the water cart and we'll get someone to dampen the dust down,' Mackie said.

By the end of the week, on our day off – or shift change as it was called – the footy game had become a highly anticipated event. To kick the big day off, a barbecue was put on, and cut-off 44-gallon drums packed with ice had been filled with free beers. Some of the boys also brought their own cartons of cans of Bundy and JDs.

At some point in the evening, they cranked up the lighting towers pinched from Boomerang pit. These lit up the playing field like a runway. By this time, the boys were all in fine form. Someone had fired up the water cart and put too much water on the footy field, so the red, powdery topsoil had turned to slop.

'Oh, well, never mind. She'll be right,' slurred Mackie.

Ed staggered on to the footy field. He was one of the digger drivers, a real hard case who had long, greying hair hanging down his back. 'Let's get this show on the road,' he yelled, looking ready to do some head banging. I reckon he might have sniffed a little something he shouldn't have.

Little Ronnie wandered over, looking as though he too might have snorted something a bit naughty.

Barney and Richie hovered over to the footy field, wearing their dark shades. They had definitely smoked something they shouldn't have. As for me, I'd drunk more than I should have.

'Right, these are the rules,' Mackie announced. 'Everyone has to be barefoot. And keep it clean. No dirty playing – all right?'

The whistle blew and Kurara versus Kanny's kicked off.

The game started off fine with everyone obeying the rules. Then suddenly I heard *twack twack!*

'Yow! That hurt,' cried a Kurara player. 'That bloke with the long hair just hit me.'

'Keep it clean, boys. Keep it clean,' bellowed Mackie.

'Oahh,' cried another Kurara player. Then, in a hoarse whisper, he gasped, 'That bloke with the long beard just winded me.'

'Come on, boys. Keep it clean. Keep it clean,' yelled Mackie.

The ball got booted out beyond the floodlights into the black of the night. I ran off into the bush, feeling around in the darkness for the ball with my bare feet. Ah, there it is! I booted it back on to the footy field, then I realised I was running around in the bush in bare feet and there were all sorts of creepy crawlies lurking around in the bush at night. Scorpions sprang to mind and I bolted out of the scrub and back onto the footy field.

The following morning, I couldn't remember who'd won the footy game. No one had stayed sober enough to keep the score. The dining room was full of the walking wounded. As I was having breakfast, I cast my eye around the room. Yep, I thought, going by the scowls on people's faces, our public relations with Kurara definitely hadn't been fixed.

* * *

Fred Riley was Kurara's mine manager and there was no love lost between him and Mackie. Riley had a big voice for a little bloke and he'd always try and get one over Mackie.

It was getting close to Christmas, and Riley turned around at the last minute and said all Kanny's staff would have to stay back at Christmas because there wasn't enough ore stockpiled up on the run-of-the-mine (ROM) pad for their loader to feed the crusher over the break. We were all gutted.

Not long after the announcement was made, Mackie drove up to my digger and waved me out of the cab. I climbed down to see what he wanted.

'Okay, Mick, this is what we're going to do. You're going to dig straight down the middle of the pit and take out all the ore that is marked out. Dig it as narrow as you can, just enough to fit the dumpies down, taking out as little waste as possible. Concentrate only on the ore. We're going to flood their ROM pad. No matter what they tell you on the radio, you keep sending those dump trucks up to the ROM pad. Got that?'

'Yeah, all good,' I replied.

When we dug out the ore, we'd usually dig across the pit. We'd start in waste rock on one side of the pit floor and dig a strip across to the middle of the pit floor where the ore body lay, which contained the gold. The ore is a seam of rock or clay and it lies on an angle of, say, 60 to 75 degrees, depending on the location of the mine.

The ore body was marked with lime powder and coloured flagging tape over the lime, so we knew what to dig out. At Kurara, red tape marked high-grade ore, yellow tape showed medium-grade ore and blue tape flagged mineral waste that was being stockpiled for possible processing later.

Once we'd dug out the ore up to the tape, from the bottom to the top of the two-and-a-half metre bench, the crust or contact should break away clean, leaving a 65-degree slope. Then we'd be back into the waste rock, which would be hauled to the waste dump.

John, the geologist, came down into the pit. His job was to spot me digging the ore. He would call out to the dump truck driver on his hand-held two-way radio, telling him the colour of the ore.

He would say something like, 'That's R for Romeo,' and hold up a red plastic disc to the dump truck driver. The driver then had to repeat, 'Copy R for Romeo,' and stick a red disc to his dashboard, to remind himself what load he was carting. This helped prevent the driver from tipping the load of ore over the waste dump by mistake. This happened from time to time, especially around knock-off when a fleet of dump trucks would tip their loads over the waste dump as they didn't want to keep the boys waiting in the Toyota Coaster bus that had been cooking in 45 degrees all day.

Having received Mackie's instructions, I cranked up and started mining the ore down the middle of the pit floor. Our dump truck drivers were steadily carting their ore up to the ROM pad and I could hear Kurara's loader driver starting to get a bit flustered, saying things like, 'Hey, bloke! You just short-dumped that load – now I have to push it up.'

I'd been digging away for about an hour, when the Kurara loader driver piped up on his two-way. 'Hey, mate, not over there. Nah! Nah!'

Too late. Up went Barney's dump tray. 'Sorry, mate, running out of room on the high-grade stockpile to tip,' he said coolly over the two-way.

'What are you doing, you mung bean?' shouted the loader driver as Richie dropped off his load at the bottom of the ramp, blocking off access to the high-grade stockpile.

'Too many rocks on the floor, mate. We don't want to slice our tyres now, do we, bloke?' Richie replied.

Pete pulled up in his dump truck.

'Just wait a moment,' screamed the loader driver.

Mackie's voice cut in over the radio. 'You dump that load, Pete!'

'Copy that. Dumping my load,' Pete responded.

'But I'm getting buried in,' the loader driver cried out.

'Then you'd better call your boss. It's not my problem,' said Mackie.

'What's going on?' Riley's hoarse voice cut in.

'Your loader's holding up my dump trucks, Riley. Sort it out,' Mackie barked.

'Well, go back on waste until the loader driver can sort it out,' Riley barked back.

'Don't tell me how to mine, Riley. You want it all by Christmas, you're getting it all by Christmas. I can hire you my dozer to keep up or I can bury your ROM pad. Either way, I don't care,' Mackie said.

Ten minutes later, our D9L dozer could be seen trundling along as it headed up to the ROM pad.

By afternoon, we were all bored out of our brains, so Barney decided to liven things up a bit. John would call out, 'That's R for Romeo.'

Barney would respond, 'Copy, that's R for rhubarb,' or 'R for radish' – pretty much any word beginning with the letter R.

We'd heard that, a couple of nights earlier, Riley had collected some of the female staff from Kurara and driven them into Meekatharra – yee-hah! – for a night out on the town. Apparently, Riley had big-noted himself in front of everyone at the pub that night.

Well, it turned out that he'd drunk one too many beersies and told one too many porkies before staggering back to his company vehicle with his female entourage in tow. He then hit the highway to drive the 80-odd k's back to camp. Unfortunately, on the way back he rolled his vehicle – thankfully, no one was injured.

Barney tried to keep us entertained with his alphabet games in an effort to stop us all nodding off. The next time John the geo called out, 'It's R for Romeo, Barney. Copy,' Barney replied, 'Copy. That's R for Riley rollover.'

But Riley, for once, was silent.

We finished up and went home for Christmas.

6
Starry, starry night

AT THE START OF wet season, I found out that my donga leaked like a sieve. I would sit and watch the water flow down the inside of my dark, simulated-woodgrain-panelled wall, over the light switch and down to the power points below. But it was home and I knew my neighbours.

After work, we would all sit down on our doorsteps and have a drink, chatting and spinning yarns, and airing out our sweaty, smelly feet. Barney usually had a tape deck playing, blaring out the likes of Van Morrison's 'Brown Eyed Girl'.

Slowly, the space underneath our dongas filled up with beer-bottle tops and cigarette butts. A quick glance under each donga and you could tell who was a drinker and who was a chain-smoker.

I reckon there were three types of blokes who worked in the mines. First, there were the druggies, who hung out together and disappeared after work to have a wee jezza or two before teatime. Later, they'd walk into the wet mess or dining room with their shades on, even though the sun had well and truly set.

The second group were the heavy drinkers, who all hung out together. They could knock back up to a dozen cans a night and if you didn't keep up with them, you were considered a fluff.

The third group, who comprised about 20 per cent of the workforce, was made up of the family men or social drinkers who didn't do drugs. The mines could be a lonely place in the evening if you wanted to chat to someone and you weren't in the 80 per cent.

A lot of blokes couldn't stand to be alone and just needed someone to talk to for company, so they would be at the wet mess every night. Some blokes couldn't handle the remoteness and would go troppo. One night, I woke to the sound of someone screaming and smashing glass. One of the kitchenhands had lost the plot and started to punch out the donga windows with his fist.

I can see how it happened. Each day, you'd wake up, get dressed then open your door at 4.30 am. Even at that time of the morning, the heat would hit you. After breakfast in the dining room – where you'd make your own crib (lunch) to take out on site with you, you'd head out to work in 40 to 45 degrees all day. When you eventually got back to camp late in the afternoon, it would still be stinking hot and it stayed that way well into the night as you tried to sleep.

A lot of the old, rattly air-cons struggled to keep you cool. There was just no escaping the heat. Outside, though, it was even worse. In the middle of the night, it could still be up to about 33 degrees. You were a prisoner to the heat. Blokes started getting claustrophobic, feeling like they were suffocating. That's when the panic set in.

One morning, I heard a commotion as the night-shift boys arrived back at camp. Out of curiosity, I poked my head out of the donga. Ed, the headbanger, was among the night-shift crew. He saw me and called out, 'Hey, Mick, Kerry's been sacked!'

'Sacked? What did he do?' I asked.

Through bursts of laughter, Ed explained. 'Well, you know how the starter motor on the bus keeps playing up? This morning it wouldn't start at all, so Kerry had a brainwave and decided to give it a push start. He had the right idea, just the wrong-sized vehicle.'

'What did he use?'

'His dump truck! He stoved the back of the bus in like he was crushing a beer can.' Ed was nearly doubled over with laughter telling me this.

I smiled. At least it meant we were finally rid of that old clanger. Maybe the new bus would have air-con …

* * *

When our day-shift crew were finally put on night shift, we went to work in Boomerang Pit, which was about 90 metres deep. This was a novelty for me as I hadn't worked in a pit at night before. Another first for me was getting to operate the old Liebherr 984 hundred-tonner. It had a slew brake, so that when I slewed the digger bucket over the tray of the dump truck, I had to put my foot on the brake to slow the turret down. If I didn't brake, I'd keep swinging past the tray and out the other side. Yee-hah!

The air-con didn't work too well, so instead I would pin back the door on the Liebherr and hack away. That was until one Sunday when I was water blasting the digger and I asked what all the light, liquorice-green-coloured dust stuck all over the pins on the boom was.

'Oh, it's just silica dust. The whole pit's full of it,' Ed said matter-of-factly.

Silica dust is now classed the same as asbestos because it can cause lung disease and silicosis.

Ed used to come into camp with his face covered in dust every day when he'd been operating that digger. Open-cast mining wasn't the healthiest environment back then.

Mining at night was a whole different ballgame. I found it hard to see properly, even though we had portable lighting towers. The towers took some time to get used to, as they cast a lot of shadows. The only good thing about night shift was that it was more relaxed. I didn't feel like we were under the microscope quite so much because all the big bosses were in bed. That was until one night when Ed was in charge.

It was about midnight and we were running out of dirt to dig. Ed didn't want to wake Mackie, but he had no choice. We all gave him stick about having to do it. Looking like he was about to face a firing squad, he drove off back to camp in his beaten-up old Tojo to wake Mackie.

A bit later, Mackie arrived on the job and hopped out of his Land Cruiser, bleary-eyed. I was waiting for him to fire up as he and Ed wandered round the pit with a torch. Finally, Mackie made his way over to me while I casually leaned against the track.

'You think this is funny, Bellamy, ruining my beauty sleep? Well, if I have to get out of bed for this, bloody Riley can, too. I've sent for him as well. He can decide where he wants us to dig. There's only one spot blasted and it's the only place to dig, but I'll get him out of bed anyway,' slurred Mackie, before he wandered off into the darkness.

* * *

When we were on night shift, Kanny's hired a new dump truck driver called Len. He was a lead foot and was always being told off for speeding down the ramp.

One night, I was digging away, listening to my Walkman cassette player, which just fitted in the top pocket of my bush shirt. I could get about eight hours out of a set of batteries, and Barney and I used to swap cassettes – my B-52s for his Guns N' Roses. Radios were banned on site, so we had to hide our Walkmans at the end of shift.

This particular night, the water cart did a run down the ramp to wet the haul road. Just as it was turning around after its run into the pit, Len's screaming voice came over the two-way: 'Get me off here. Get me off. Help! Help!' He was hysterical.

As I was looking around the pit for Len, Ed's voice cut in on the radio: 'Hey, Mick, get your digger away from the wall of the pit and walk it out into the middle of the floor, mate. Quick as you can ... and don't look up.'

Of course, the first thing I did was look up. At first, all I saw was a cloudless, desert sky with its bright twinkling stars. About 90 metres above me, I noticed two stars moving up and down slowly. I took a second glance, thinking it was my imagination. Yep, there were definitely two stars moving up and down. What the hell was going on up there?

'Hurry up, Mick, and get that digger out of there,' Ed yelled.

'Shit! That's a 777 dump truck hanging over the edge above me,' I cried out. It was see-sawing on the windrow, the mound of dirt used as a barrier to stop vehicles from driving over the edge.

Len had sped down the ramp just after the water cart had gone down, so the haul road descending into the pit was slippery. Len lost control of his 777 and hit the high wall at speed, which damaged his steering and fired his dump truck back towards the 90-metre drop-off, with only a windrow of dirt stopping him from going right over the edge.

His dump truck had come to an abrupt halt, see-sawing right on top of the windrow, as Len looked out into blackness, unable to climb down the back of the tray because it was too high off the ground.

Luckily, the D9L dozer was up at the waste dump, so Reg brought it down to the top of the pit where he quickly hooked it up to the 777 and towed it backwards, off the edge. If the dozer had been working down in the pit, it would have been cut off by the dump truck across the haul road and the outcome for Len would have been much less positive.

Len was a wreck as he climbed down the ladder and off the dump truck. He refused a lift and walked all the way back to camp in darkness.

The next day, there was a marathon windrow building session. The rule of thumb is: a windrow should be half the tyre height of the biggest dump truck on site – in our case, the hundred-tonne 777, but our windrows had been built for the 50-tonne dump trucks before the 777s arrived on site.

7
Southern Cross

THEY WERE A GOOD bunch of blokes to work with at Kurara, but when the night shift got scaled back it meant one of the crew would have to go. It was down to me or one of the two other digger drivers, both of whom had girlfriends working on site in the camp. Being the only single bloke, I put my hand up for a transfer to Southern Cross, which suited me fine.

One thing about Kurara I definitely wouldn't miss was the communal toilet and shower block arrangement. There were six toilet cubicles in a row, then six shower cubicles right next to them. In their wisdom, whoever designed the toilet block put the washbasins right in front of the toilet doors. In the morning, when you were bent over the washbasin, trying to brush your teeth, some big, hairy miner would be right behind you, sitting on the toilet, having a smoke, hocking, spitting and farting to the sound of plop-plop-plop. This made it hard to brush your gnashers without gagging.

* * *

Southern Cross was created around Fraser Mine. It was the site of the first major gold discovery in the Eastern Goldfields in 1887. The goldrush in Coolgardie followed in 1892 and at Kalgoorlie a year later.

Southern Cross was only about three-and-a-half hours' drive east from Perth and a bit over halfway to Kalgoorlie. They didn't work six weeks on, one week off there either, so I'd get to go back to Perth every second weekend. It sounded too good to be true – and it was.

I got a lift up to Southern Cross with Calvin, the dirt boss. The camp was right in Southern Cross township and the dongas were tucked in behind the pub.

A bloke once told me, 'Mick, I reckon after about three days you can generally tell if you're going to stick around or snatch it.' And he was right. From the start, I didn't like the place. It just didn't have the camp camaraderie I was used to.

When I arrived out at Fraser Pit, the mine was running a new 984 Leibherr, an old CAT 245, an old Hitachi EX1000 excavator and seven old CAT 777B dump trucks. I got the impression most of the crew were smart arses. Probably because it was so close to Perth, the place had a city-folk mentality, whereas up in the bush, they were a good bunch who soon sorted out the idiots and the smart arses.

I drove the EX1000, which couldn't pull the skin off a rice pudding even though it had two engines. The ground was like schist, slabby and locked together. With some of it, I couldn't even dig the bench in strips. It was literally crossways, sideways, backways – whatever worked. So, I was back to chipping and scraping again. The hard ground was cracking the welds on the bucket.

Two mornings in a row, I had to pick up the digger from the workshop after night shift had destroyed it, then tram the digger all the way back to the pit, which lost me time and productivity.

One morning, I heard the young bloke who drove my digger on night shift outside my donga door. He clearly didn't realise it was my donga as he said, 'That new digger driver is hopeless. I've beaten him two nights in a row for moving dirt. What's he doing?'

Well, I didn't need to hear that first thing in the morning. I opened the door and said, 'Well, if you didn't keep breaking the bucket, you tosser, I might just stand a chance. Any more crap out of you and I'll bang you over the head with your schoolbag!'

He just stood there, looking sheepish.

Right in the middle of the floor of Fraser Pit was an old mineshaft dating back to the late 1800s. It was one of the first underground mines in the Eastern Goldfields region. Up beside one of the waste dumps was a mountain of old mine props, heaped up in piles, finally seeing the light of day, having been underground for over 100 years. Loads that were contaminated with these mine props had to be sent to a rehandle area because nothing but ore was allowed to go through the crushers.

I found the underground shafts fascinating. There were dark holes up in the open pit walls where the old mineshafts had been daylighted. Apparently, they'd even found an old smoko room down there.

One morning, I was digging away, half asleep, having just finished loading a dump truck. I gave a toot on the air horn and the old dump truck pulled away in a cloud of smoke. Then it slowed down and nearly stopped when its left-hand back wheels dropped down a hole that had appeared from nowhere. Nearly tipping over, the dump truck kept moving slowly while producing an even bigger cloud of smoke as the engine laboured its guts out. Somehow, the driver managed to pull it out of the hole before carrying on out of the pit.

Moments later, the pit floor opened up before me and water boiled up out of the ground. At the time, I thought I must have broken a big water main. Then I realised I was 30 metres down a pit – I was definitely not in the city now!

As water slowly flooded the pit floor, I realised the 777 had dropped into an old mineshaft. I'd never really thought about it, but it made sense that all the old mineshafts would be full of groundwater since they were below the water table level.

Typical of back then, management just banged four skinny pegs around the hole in the ground, added some pink flagging tape and – hey presto – it was all nice and safe.

At lunchtime that day, Tony, the fitter, came up to me and said, 'Hey, Mick, just leave her running, mate. Got to do a bit of work on the old girl.'

'No worries, Tony,' I said, as I climbed out of the cab.

At lunchtime, I was sitting outside the office block eating my sandwiches when I heard someone call out, 'Hey, Mick, you've got to go see Calvin in his office.'

Immediately, there was a chorus of oohs and aahs and some finger-wagging.

I wandered over to the office and banged on Calvin's door. 'You want to see me?'

'I don't want to see that digger idling by itself ever again, Mick. Do I make myself clear? You shut it off at lunchtime – got it?' he drawled, in his broad South African accent.

'I was told to leave it idling by a fitter,' I replied, without naming names.

'Don't give me your made-up excuses,' Calvin roared.

'Tell you what, Calvin, how about you poke your idling digger up your date? Do I make myself clear?' I said, then walked out.

Life was an adventure: I was single and Western Australia was a big state with plenty to explore. The way I saw it, I'll treat you the same way you treat me.

My mate Nick from Wiluna was living back in Perth, so I gave him a call and told him what had happened.

'You want a scraper job?' he asked. 'Leightons are looking for scraper drivers and I just got a start.'

I'd only ever driven an old Terex scraper on the North Shore of Auckland, working on a highway job building Constellation Drive – and my ears were still ringing from it.

When I told Nick this, he said, 'You'll be right. Nothing to it. Be good for a laugh.'

I hitched a ride back to Perth the following day. There, I stayed with Nick and his family, which was my home away from home. Awesome family.

Next morning, Nick drove me into the city to meet Brad, the personnel manager at Leightons. Brad was just like Ken from Kanny's. Personnel managers always seemed to have the same look about them – tired, withdrawn, quiet spoken and generally long-suffering, with dark rings around their eyes, a bit like an undertaker in a Wild West movie.

I was prepared when Brad asked me what experience I had. 'Well, I've driven a Terex scraper. It was an old clanger, but it went like the clappers,' I said.

'That's good,' he said, and laughed. 'A scraper is a scraper. I've got a six-week job at Mulgarrie taking the first 60 feet off the top of a new pit. When can you start?'

A couple of days later, Nick and I hopped on the Prospector train to Kalgoorlie. It was pretty modern for its day: reclining seats, nice air-con. It even had a trolley service giving out food and alcohol in miniature spirit bottles, which is probably why I don't remember much of the journey!

After getting off the train in Kalgoorlie in the late afternoon, Nick and I staggered off the platform to find a taxi. I was surprised how big Kal was – it was a city in the middle of nowhere.

It was easy to tell that it was a mining town. Red-stained four-wheel drives were parked everywhere, each with the logo of a mining company on its doors. Old headframes from the original underground mining operations were scattered along the Golden Mile. Most of these had been shut down ready for the open cut Super Pit to swallow them up.

I was fascinated by it all.

If you took all the vehicles away, the place would look like it did 100 years ago. I could imagine the early prospectors' horses and carts driving down the streets and their horses hitched up outside the Exchange Hotel, which still had the original batwing doors. I could almost feel the history of the place and sense the ghosts of the early prospectors wandering the streets.

We stayed at a camp in Boulder, which is at the southern end of the Golden Mile. The camp was nothing to rave about. It was out in a paddock down a long gravel road on the edge of Boulder. It was surrounded by dead grass, bits of old, rusted corrugated iron, rusty tin cans and it had a beautiful view of all the waste dumps along the Golden Mile. Lovely!

The following day, we caught up with some of the other scraper drivers, Rangi and Cliff, over a beer. They were both good blokes in their twenties, but Cliff was a bit older than Rangi and he was quietly spoken. Rangi was the complete opposite. I'm not sure whether he was outgoing or out of it – probably both.

Also at the table was Mark, who usually worked as a shotfirer but was on compo. We didn't get much out of him as he'd just drunk a bottle of Wild Turkey. If the drool running down his chin and the fact he was holding his head in his hands were anything to go by, he wasn't feeling the best. There were also little bits of skin missing off his hands, which had scabbed over.

'Hey, Mark, how did you wind up on compo?' I asked.

He opened one bleary, bloodshot eye and slurred, 'Bit embarrassed to tell you …'

'Come on, Mark,' boomed Nick. 'We won't laugh, mate.'

'Well, well, I blew myself up,' Mark mumbled.

'Blew yourself up?' Nick burst into fits of laughter, joined by the rest of us. 'I suppose playing with explosives will do that to a man from time to time! Light the wrong end, mate?'

Mark just shook his head and passed out.

We had a look at the roster they had made up that afternoon. All of us were on night shift the next evening. We hopped on our Toyota Coaster bus and headed out of Kal to Mulgarrie.

At the mine, they had four CAT 631Es, four 651E CAT scrapers, one D10N and one D11N dozer. Me, Rangi, Cliff and a local bloke, Tim, were on the smaller 631E scrapers and our dozer operator Keith drove the D10N. Nick drove one of the 651Es and his dozer operator was called D9. When I met that bloke and he introduced himself, he drawled slowly, 'Yeah, I'm Dee Niiine.'

What sort of bloke would name himself after a bulldozer? A prima donna with a big Caterpillar belt buckle and a brand-new Caterpillar jacket, that's what sort.

'How come they call you D9 when you drive a D11?' I asked him while trying to keep a straight face. My question fell on deaf ears.

He was your typical dozer operator of the era. He had a big, fat beer gut that hung over his big CAT belt buckle, rubbing it shiny. Our dozer driver Keith was cast from the same mould. One too many beers at the wettie every night for years had turned him into a fine specimen of a man. He was a quiet bloke with squinty eyes, which gave the impression he needed to go somewhere quickly.

Driving the scraper at Mulgarrie provided a steep learning curve for me. The mining operation was run like Bathurst. When the bus arrived on site, my scraper would be parked up waiting for me, already checked over and idling away. All I had to do was climb up in the seat and chase my mate down the haul road, full noise. His job was to push-load the scraper, which meant driving up behind it with his dozer at an angle then swinging on to the back of my push pad with his big blade, making contact as smoothly as possible and pushing the scraper until it was full of dirt. The scraper operator would then lift his bowl up and pull away from the dozer. But if the dozer driver loved to have a jezza or two or sniffed something a bit naughty and was high as a kite, which in the case of my dozer driver was most of the time, I'd be in for a long night.

If the dozer driver stuffed up with his dozer swinging on to the scraper, I'd get 56 tonnes of bulldozer slamming up my rear end, which pretty much knocked me round like a rag doll in the cab. It could give me instant whiplash, but – worst case scenario – it could have broken my spine. Similarly, if the driver was to flat-blade me at speed and didn't swing in at an angle, the scenario would be the same … or possibly worse.

One night, Keith smacked my scraper so hard that the transmission jammed in low gear, and I had to limp back to the workshop. The scrapers were nearly new, under 500 hours old. It goes to show what rough operating can do.

Another of Keith's dirty tricks was to pick the rear end of the scraper up as high as he could with his big blade, then suddenly let the scraper drop back on its wheels. Inside the cab, I'd be almost torn in half by my lap belt. The mines were all about construction and management turned a blind eye to this sort of thing – you were just a number.

8

Rangi's reefer

WE WERE ON OUR way back to camp in our Toyota Coaster bus one morning when we pulled up outside a pub on the outskirts of Kal.

'What pub opens at 6.30?' asked Nick as he peered out of the bus window.

'One that caters for shift workers,' said Cliffy.

'Well, this is a first for me. I can't say I've been to a pub at 6.30 in the morning before!' I observed.

We all piled into the pub, which smelt of stale beer and ashtrays. It was dark and dingy and my boots stuck to the floor. We ordered a round of beers and a cider for Cliffy because he thought that was cool.

A couple of hours later, Nick was cracking jokes and the boys were unwinding from night shift and starting to get a bit boisterous. We even got a nod from Cliffy because it was cool to nod.

At about 11 o'clock, we piled back into the bus and headed into Kal. We didn't get far before the bus pulled up outside the Foundry Hotel. We all piled out of the bus and into the pub. We ordered another round of beers and a cider for Cliffy, who gave us his coolest nod.

By about seven that evening, we were still at the Foundry. Through glazed eyes I peered around the room and all I could see was a sea of big, hairy miners who wouldn't win any beauty contests and a crowd of bikies who had faces only a mother would love. And then there was Cliffy, still holding onto his composure, coolly sipping on his cider and leaning against the bar. I could hear Nick's booming laugh as he told yet another yarn. Rangi was still standing too, but I was just about nodding off on my feet.

By about 9 pm, Nick had quietened down a bit. Rangi's eyes had puffed out and he had a silly grin on his dial – possibly because he'd been outside for a sneaky puff of something with one of the bikies – and Cliffy was holding his cider and staring out into space, still looking cool. Meanwhile, I'd developed a major speech impediment.

By closing time, the place was chocka. Having lost sight of Rangi and Cliffy, Nick and I decided to try to walk the five k's back to Boulder. As we staggered down the street, I found an abandoned shopping trolley and Nick proceeded to climb into it for a laugh. I pushed him in the shopping trolley along the footpath for about half a block down Boulder Road. Then I ran out of steam. Nick was a big bloke, so it was like trying to push a beached whale.

'Come on, Mick, you fluff, push!' his voice boomed out into the darkness.

'Don't call me a fluff, you beached whale,' I said, and laughed.

Scratching the stubble on his chin, Nick said, 'This is going to be a mission, climbing out of this contraption.'

By then, he was stuck in the shopping trolley with his fat, hairy legs dangling out over the front.

'Nah, I've got an idea,' I replied, grinning as I pushed the trolley off the footpath and over the kerb.

'Aagh! Mick, you bastard,' was all I heard before a loud metal clang rang out through the darkness and the shopping trolley tipped over on its side.

Nick unceremoniously rolled out onto Boulder Road, then he staggered back on to his feet, brushed himself off, pointed up the road and said, 'Hey, Mick, isn't that Rangi standing over by those trees?'

I tried to focus my bleary eyes. 'I can see two Rangis standing there.'

Nick called out, 'Hey, Rangi, you okay, mate?'

'Yeah, just waiting for Cliffy,' he answered. 'He just ducked behind those bushes. Been gone a while, though.'

We stood there under the stars on a warm desert night trying to chat, which was a bit hard given we'd been drinking since 6.30 that morning and it was now around midnight – and we'd all just come off night shift.

Suddenly, we heard shrieks of laughter coming from a group of four girls who had come from the other side of the bushes.

'Hey, you blokes waiting for your mate?' one girl asked while laughing hysterically. 'You'll be waiting a long time. You'd better go and have a look at him!' This was followed by gales of laughter from her friends as they wandered off into the night.

'Hey, Cliffy, you all right, mate?' I called out.

No answer.

'Hey, Nick, go have a look for him in those bushes,' I said.

'Bugger off. You go, Mick!'

'Nah, I'm still seeing double …'

'All right, all right, I'll go, or we'll be here all night,' Rangi muttered, as he wandered off into the bushes.

A few moments later, Rangi's voice rang out of the darkness. 'Hey, guys, come and have a look at this.'

Nick and I rustled through a few bushes then popped out on the other side of a clearing. Poor old Cliffy wasn't looking so cool now. He must have got caught short, dropped his daks, then passed out halfway through and toppled backwards. The funniest thing was, that on the other side of the bushes was a busy intersection, so half the cars waiting to turn got a bird's-eye view of poor Cliffy lying there with his jeans down around his ankles, his lily-white knees shining in the moonlight as he snored loudly.

We did what all good mates would do – we pretended not to know him and quietly snuck off down the road, sniggering away to ourselves. There were no cell phones with cameras in those days, or we would have had a ball.

The next day was our day off. Nick banged on my donga door and woke me up.

'Get out of bed, you lazy sod,' his voice boomed out. He opened my donga door and said, 'Hey, Mick, do you want to see an underground mine along the Golden Mile? It's a tourist attraction.'

'Yeah, why not?' I replied. 'I've never been underground.'

Shortly afterwards, a taxi dropped us off at the Hainault Gold Mine. (Unfortunately, it has been swallowed up by the Kalgoorlie Super Pit now and is long gone.)

Inside, the staff took us into a little room and issued us each with a hard hat with a lamp on it. Then we climbed into a lift cage and the guide took us down about 60 metres below the big headframe, where he showed us the workings of the mine.

The guide dropped a beer can down a reef where the vein of ore had been mined. It was now a dark crevasse. Ting ting ting, we heard, as the can bounced off the reef walls hundreds of metres below until the sound faded slowly away. The guide shone his torch on the wall of the reef. Gold was still visible in the wall.

We walked along another mineshaft. There were no lights in a working pit in those days: just the lamp on your head. The guide showed us the grizzly where they tipped the ore down. In a working mine in those days, there were no barricades to stop anyone from falling in the deep, dark hole all the way down to the bottom of the pit. The hole might descend to a depth of more than 300 metres. After the ore was tipped into the hole, it would be taken to the lift. The big headframes littered the Golden Mile.

The miners worked hard back then. The guide gave us a demonstration on the air leg drill, which was a drill on a stand. It was so loud I could have yelled in Nick's ear and he wouldn't have heard a word I said.

It was a great experience being a tourist, but I was happy to see the light of day as the cage door opened for us. It takes a special person to work underground and I decided it wasn't for me.

On Sunday night, we got back on the bus to go back to Mulgarrie for the start of a new shift. Keith had a new dirty trick for me that night. After he'd pushed the last scraper in one direction, when it was my turn to be pushed, he came up behind me. I was expecting to go in the same direction as the other scrapers, but the corner of his blade suddenly changed direction and he started pushing me sideways until I jack-knifed the scraper. Then he stopped and reversed out, leaving me there like an idiot. What was that all about?

At smoko, I asked the boys if Keith had done the same to them. They were all experienced scraper drivers.

'He's tried it, Mick,' said Cliffy, 'but I won't let him. If he tried it again, be ready to quickly lift your bowl and turn the front of the scraper real quick, so he can't jack-knife you.'

Sure enough, after smoko, Keith tried it again. So, up with the bowl. I swung the turret of the scraper hard around, accelerated hard and, yep, it worked. Keith stopped trying that trick again, but I had to keep an eye on him: give him an inch, he'd take a mile.

* * *

I found it hardest to stay awake at about three o'clock in the morning, especially on the first night of the shift. We were all driving flat out, chasing each other as usual, and I had just emptied my load down the side of the waste dump before turning back onto the haul road, where I floored it.

The CAT V8 motor was screaming as the transmission changed, hunting up through the gears until it hit top gear then away I went, tearing off down the haul road.

By three o'clock, I'd started daydreaming and my mind had wandered off. I had one last, sharp bend in the haul road, which came out at the top of the ramp and ran about 20 metres feet down to the pit floor. The last corner itself wasn't a problem. In the dry, I could barrel around it, hardly buttoning off on the accelerator at all.

This night, I came flying up to the last corner and suddenly noticed, in the beam of my headlights, that the haul road was shiny. The day crew had sheeted the road with the wrong material! This woke me up instantly as I noticed the rear end of my scraper sliding round to meet me.

Not good! In a motor scraper the bowl is your brake, so – in an emergency – if you drop the bowl, it will pull you up in an instant. But if you drop the bowl too quickly, you'll wind up kissing the windscreen or dashboard, which will provide you with a nasty lump on your noggin. On the other hand, if you panic and drop the bowl as it starts to slide or jack-knife on you, the corner of the bowl will dig into the ground and you will roll the scraper over onto its roof, in which case you will definitely get a nasty lump on your noggin – and probably be out of a job.

I tried to accelerate and straighten the scraper, but I had left it too late. On one side, at the top of the ramp was a lighting tower. On the other side of the ramp, the leading hand, Derek, was parked up leaning over the bonnet of his Land Cruiser, using the lights to read his plans.

There was nothing I could do as I came out of the bend. The scraper was 14 metres long, completely sideways and heading for poor old Derek and the lighting tower.

Everything was happening in slow motion. I turned the turret of the scraper at the last minute to narrow up the gap as I slid past, missing Derek and the lighting tower by centimetres.

Derek looked up, shook his head and returned to reading his plans as if nothing had happened. I then spun around down at the bottom of the ramp and wound up facing the other way. I found out later that the water cart driver had forgotten to turn off his sprays on the bend. He was probably half asleep like the rest of us.

Near the end of the week, Keith's dozer broke down. It was about eight o'clock in the evening when Leightons' dirt boss showed up to sort it out. He was standing beside the big front tyre of Rangi's scraper, down beside his cab while I was parked right behind the scraper.

It was dark by then, and Rangi and I were just sitting in our cabs, waiting for them to sort out the dozer. I was drumming my fingers on the steering wheel, and I gazed up at the stars, twinkling away on another clear, warm evening. It was relaxing just to sit there looking at the majestic Southern Cross and studying the desert night sky – far better than listening to a screaming V8 CAT scraper motor all evening.

As I stared out into the night, I caught sight of another light out of the corner of my eye. It was Rangi turning on the light in his cab. He was fossicking around, looking for something in his crib bag. Then – lo and behold! He pulled out this huge joint the size of a cigar, popped it in his gob, lit it and had a huge choof before exhaling and giving me a big thumbs up over his shoulder. He then disappeared in a cloud of smoke and turned his cab light off.

I cracked up laughing while watching the dirt boss standing just below Rangi's cab, oblivious to what was going on above him. It was probably the first time I realised that two of the scraper drivers were high as kites, and two other scraper drivers on that shift had drunk a carton each during the day, instead of sleeping, and were legless. One took a taxi from Kalgoorlie to work and the other, a local, took his own car to work, which was an hour's drive. These were the guys who spent each night chasing me around, tailgating me in 78 tonnes of loaded scraper just for a laugh.

At 5.30 am, we all piled into our trusty Toyota Coaster bus. We had survived another week of being bashed about by a redneck and were looking forward to having a day off. This time, instead of stopping at the pub, we went straight back to our camp in Boulder.

I hopped off the bus when we got there and quietly snuck off in the opposite direction to the rest of the boys – my plan being to avoid getting on the booze first thing in the morning. So far so good as I popped into the camp dining room for a quick brekkie without being noticed. Then I snuck over to the shower block without being spotted. I darted out with a towel round my waist and snuck past all the boys, who were starting to be boisterous. I could hear the sounds of tops popping from their stubbies.

Whew! I had made it back to my donga without being sprung, so I jumped into bed in my jocks and blissfully dozed off to sleep.

Bang, bang, bang! I was woken by someone knocking on my door, then I heard Nick's booming voice echoing down the corridor: 'Mick – hey, Mick – wake up, you fluff.'

He opened my donga door. 'Oh, were you asleep?' he asked. 'Never mind. You're awake now! I brought your favourite beer.' He held up two six-packs of Redback. 'You'd better have one so they don't get warm,' he added, fluttering his eyelashes, which wasn't a pretty sight to wake up to.

I reluctantly propped myself up in bed and pulled the sheet up around my waist.

'Look, I've even opened it for you, Mick,' Nick said, handing me a stubbie of Redback as he parked his big frame on the end of my bed. 'I ordered them yesterday at the wet mess.'

I rummaged in my bedside draw for my stubbie holder, then looked up to see Rangi's ugly dial poking around my donga door.

'Oh, are you fellas having a beer? Mind if I join you?' he asked.

'Nah, not at all. Grab a pew,' Nick boomed.

Rangi plonked himself down on the floor with his back against the wall, then Nick started telling us a yarn. Later, Cliffy popped his head round the door, took one look at me sitting up in bed with no top on and cracked up laughing. He pulled a chair up outside the donga door and, using his lighter, flicked the top off a cider bottle and had a swig.

Nick carried on entertaining us through the morning. By about 10 o'clock, it was a full-on session. A couple of road-train drivers and an RC driller had joined Cliffy, and they were sitting in a semi-circle of chairs outside my donga door.

By 11 o'clock, I was thinking, Man, this is another first for me: I'm full as a boot and I haven't even got out of bed yet.

Nick was in full swing: 'Hey, Rangi, do you want a bet? Are you man or mouse?'

'What kind of bet?' Rangi asked, suspiciously. He was sitting on the floor with his legs straight out in front when Nick poured a bit of his beer onto the floor between Rangi's knees.

Nick got down on his knees between Rangi's ankles then handed Rangi one of my thongs. 'Okay, Rangi, the bet is that I can wipe up that spilt beer between your legs with a towel without you clobbering my hand with that thong.'

Rangi beamed. 'Too easy.'

Nick's started hovering with the hand towel, making out he was going to have a crack at wiping up the beer. Rangi took a vicious swipe at Nick's hand and just missed it with the thong.

Nick made out he was having another crack at wiping up the beer, by leaning a bit further forward and waving his hand towel, with Rangi's thong just missing Nick's hand to a chorus of cheers from us.

Nick's voice boomed out, 'Remember the bet is for me to wipe up that beer.'

'Yeah, yeah, I'm hearing you,' Rangi replied, fully focused on Nick's hand.

'Good,' Nick said, as he leaned forward again and did a dummy pass.

Rangi swiped out at Nick's hand once again.

Nick suddenly grabbed Rangi by the ankles and pulled his body straight through the puddle of beer.

'I won, I won,' Nick shouted, to the sound of laughter from the boys.

Rangi's cries of 'That's cheating! That's cheating!' went ignored through the fits of laughter as he stood up with a wet bum.

* * *

The Boulder Block Hotel did a two-for-the-price-of-one deal on Sundays, so one Sunday our crew headed down there. The place was packed but we managed to squeeze our way in.

While waiting to be served at the bar, I noticed a big metal grate over the dance floor. As I walked back to our table with my drinks, I stopped to have a peep through the grate. All I could see was a big hole leading into blackness. A mineshaft!

How cool is that? I bet there's not too many pubs around with mineshafts *in* their dance floors.

The Boulder Block Hotel was located south of Kal, along the Golden Mile. Even back in the 1800s, the acre of land known as the Boulder Block had a shady reputation, being home to houses of ill repute, hotels and dubious characters from all walks of life.

There are all sorts of stories about the mineshaft in the cellar, such as miners illegally bringing up the gold ore from the shaft to sell to willing customers in the bar. It was six months' hard labour if a miner was caught selling gold at the pub in the late 1800s.

After our session at the Boulder Block, we were walking across the road and suddenly heard shouts and arguing. A bouncer had just chucked a young bloke out on the footpath.

The young bloke got up and said something to the gorilla of a bouncer, then walked off up the street, but he kept on abusing the bouncer over his shoulder as he walked off.

Unfortunately, the young bloke swore one too many times at this big gorilla of a bouncer, who casually walked up behind the young bloke – and I'll always remember the sound of the meaty slap as the bouncer king-hit him – *Whack!* And down fell the young bloke.

A rough town and rough justice.

A year after our session at the pub, the Boulder Block Hotel was demolished to make way for the Super Pit. Only the ghosts of the past remain: the history of the dirty acre loaded out by a face shovel.

* * *

At work the night after our Sunday session, my back was still playing up from all Keith's rough push-loading with his dozer. I was surprised he hadn't broken it, given all the times the back of my seat had slammed into my kidneys and spine, often leaving me winded – Keith was that brutal.

When I talked to Cliffy about it one night, he'd said, 'Mick, there's a dirty trick you can do back at him ...' He went on to explain what I could do, before grinning and adding, 'It's a last resort but it will sharpen his act up.'

Around midnight on our next night shift, we'd eaten our 'lunch' and I could tell Keith was in a foul mood. I reckoned he'd probably run out of weed, as he was bashing the living daylights out of me with his dozer.

I started to get really brassed off – my back was killing me and I could feel every bump I drove over. Every time Keith came sailing in on his dozer, I would tense up, waiting for the inevitable impact as his blade smashed into the rear end of my scraper.

'Right, just you wait for the next round,' I muttered as I limped off to dump my load.

I slowly climbed up and over the waste dump, emptying my load out of the bowl as I went. My back was in a bad way.

I headed back down the pit into our cut area. My usual routine was to drag my bowl through the cut until it was part filled. Then I would pull to a halt and wait for the dozer to swing in and push me through. This time, though, I pulled up empty and left my bowl just clearing the ground while I waited. It wasn't long before Keith came sailing up behind me

As soon as he came into sight, I muttered, 'This is going to bloody hurt!'

I gritted my teeth, whacked my scraper into reverse and floored it straight backwards like a battering ram until I slammed all 43 tonnes of my scraper into his dozer blade. Keith's head and the top half of his body slammed towards his window like a rag doll.

'Take that, you clown,' I said.

But I was still really brassed off. I knew the impact had now poked my back completely. I got out of my scraper. Keith hadn't noticed, so he kept pushing my scraper. It was fairly dark in that corner of the pit. I let him push the scraper over a bank and watched the door on the scraper swinging like a dunny door in the wind, back and forth.

I could see Keith squinting out of his window, wondering what was going on, until he looked around and saw me standing right beside his track with a handful of rocks, ready to smash out his windows.

He stopped the dozer and I climbed up the track to haul him out of his cab. But he had locked himself in. I could see the whites of his eyes as he peered out through the dust-stained glass, looking, this time, like he really needed to go somewhere desperately. Even over the noise of his idling dozer, I could hear his muffled voice cry out, 'You're bloody mad!'

He'd got the message. I climbed down and hobbled over to my scraper. It was the end of shift and the end of the job for me.

When Nick found out what had happened, he told them to stick their job as well.

In the morning, Nick had to carry my suitcase. I couldn't even lift it onto the train back to Perth.

9

A session with a good ole boy

I DECIDED TO HAVE a crack at working in Perth as I'd never worked there before. The first thing I needed to do was get a set of wheels to get around in. I bought an old Ford Cortina station wagon off Nick's sister-in-law for $500. It was an automatic. If I accelerated too hard, a wave of exhaust smoke would roll out in front of the dashboard and almost asphyxiate me.

The next thing I did was apply for a flat in Beaconsfield, close to Fremantle. It was described as 'a three-bedroomed character home', although I would call it 'a dump'. But it was a foot in the door.

My two flatmates were Len, who was training to be a chef, and Chloe, who was a uni student. Len and I got on well, and we'd head down to Fremantle on Sundays for a session at either the Sail and Anchor or at a little bar at the Fremantle

Markets. Later in the day, we'd stagger home, where we would drink Chloe's legendary home brew.

One Friday night, I was down at the Sail and Anchor having a Redback with Nick. A big American aircraft carrier had just docked at Fremantle, so the bar was full of American sailors. My flatmate Len hated American sailors. Being born and bred in Freo, he saw them as competition for the local girls, so he and his mates would often pick fights with them when they came to town.

One of the sailors walked up to the bar that Nick and I were propping up. Nick took one look at him and burst out laughing. I turned to see what was so funny – and here's this American sailor wearing an Akubra stockman's hat. There's nothing wrong with that – heaps of Aussie blokes wear Akubra hats.

He was also wearing a nice pair of RM Williams leather boots. Again, nothing wrong with that – he was pouring his money into the Australian economy.

To top it off, he was wearing a brand-new, ankle-length Driza-Bone oilskin raincoat, which made him look dashing – just like the Man from Snowy River, all dressed up for those cold, bitter, wintery nights. The only problem was, it was a stinking hot summer's evening and everyone else was in tee-shirts, shorts and thongs. Yee-hah!

Nick stopped laughing and said to the sailor, 'Howdy, partner.'

Well, the sailor's eyes lit up and he answered back in a Texas drawl, 'Well, howdy y'all. Hi, I'm Bobby from Texas.'

'Really? I wouldn't have guessed,' replied Nick as he shook Bobby's hand.

We struck up a conversation with Bobby, trying to make him feel at home, but his eyes were darting all round the pub. He was not really interested in what we had to say, as he was more interested in the opposite sex.

A bit later on, Nick was in full debate mode as his voice boomed out above the noise of the crowd at the bar: 'Yeah, Bobby, but we've got the most poisonous snakes in the world.'

'No, Nick, you can't beat our western diamondback rattlesnake,' Bobby said adamantly.

'Bull! Our inland taipan can kill a horse, so beat that,' Nick said, with a thump of his fist on the bar.

'Don't get your cows runnin', Nick,' said Bobby.

'My cows what?'

Bobby laughed. 'It means "relax".'

Apparently, according to Bobby, everything's bigger and better in Texas. Speaking of bigger, I couldn't help but notice that, under his big oilskin coat, which was undone at the front, Bobby was wearing this huge – and I mean huge – round belt buckle. It looked like the sort of buckle a wrestler wins in a title fight.

'Hey, Bobby,' I said. 'What's that huge belt buckle you're wearing, mate? It looks like a hubcap.'

He proudly opened his coat to show us. 'We all wear these here belt buckles back home.'

'Whose HQ Holden did you pinch that off, Bobby?' Nick asked.

Bobby looked confused. 'HQ what?'

Nick started laughing. 'Crikey, Bobby, that looks like my poor old grandma's tea tray hanging off your belt.'

'What's so funny?' Bobby asked.

'It's okay, mate. We're just taking a lend of ya,' I said.

'A what?'

'A lend of you – taking the mickey out of you,' I explained.

'Mickey, who's Mickey?'

'Never mind, Bobby. Just pulling your leg, mate. A joke.' Then I asked, 'So, what's your job on the aircraft carrier? Are you a jet fighter pilot maybe?'

'No, I'm the coffee percolator attendant,' he replied.

'Shit, that sounds really important,' Nick said, trying – and failing – to keep a straight face.

Soon, we bade farewell to Bobby and wished him good luck in his travels.

After closing time, I got in my old Ford Cortina station wagon and was driving home when, suddenly, in the headlights I saw this big African-American sailor waving his arms at me to stop.

I pulled over.

'You okay, mate?' I asked.

'I'm a US Mah-rine and I'm lost. I have this phone number to ring and they will collect me,' he said, in a way that implied it was my duty to give him a ride.

I thought about it for a second then grinned as I imagined what would happen if I took this bloke back to my flat for Len to meet ...

'Yeah, of course. Jump in, buddy,' I said, thinking this was going to be a laugh. 'I live just round the corner. You can use our home phone, mate.'

Len wasn't home when we arrived, so I popped the top off one of Chloe's home-brewed beers and plonked it down on the table.

'Sorry, I didn't introduce myself. I'm Mike,' I said.

'I'm Forest,' he said, as we shook hands.

The front door banged open and Len walked in, muttering and cursing. 'Bloody Yanks are everywhere. Where are you, Mick?'

'I'm in the kitchen, mate. We have a guest,' I called out.

'Oh,' Len said, as he poked his head round the door. He was sporting a big black eye. He'd obviously met his match with some American sailor and was not a happy chappy, especially when he clamped eyes on Forest.

'Hey, Len. Meet my new buddy, Forest. He's a US Mah-rine,' I said, beaming from ear to ear.

The black eye must have done the trick, as the rest of Forest's visit went without incident and Len eventually forgave me.

* * *

I met up with Nick one Saturday morning and we went for a drive out to Willagee to visit an old mate of Nick's called Dennis. It turned out he knew my sister back when they were kids in the seventies. Small world.

When I first knew him, Dennis had been a real larrikin and nothing much had changed. He hadn't lost his sense of humour, but he was missing his long hair and bellbottoms, although he still managed to give the impression he had just been to Woodstock.

We chatted about old times, then Dennis offered to show me his garden.

Grinning to myself and thinking he was probably growing things he shouldn't, I followed him out into his backyard. It was like a jungle out there, but it was full of amazing plants and vegetables in among wind chimes and garden statues. He was definitely a good gardener.

'Hey, Dennis, these are colourful,' I said, pointing at some of his plants.

He laughed. 'They're chillies, Mick! They might look bright and cheerful, but they're dynamite to eat. I consider myself a chilli connoisseur, as I've got cast-iron guts – or so I thought. The other day I wolfed a couple of them down,' he said, throwing his hands in the air. 'I thought I was going to die.'

The chillies weren't much bigger than an oval vitamin pill.

'Oh, wow, I've never seen a chilli plant before,' I said. 'Such bright colours, aren't they?'

'Do you want some? I've got a heap of them inside if you want.'

'I wouldn't touch them with a barge pole,' Nick's voice boomed out from behind some tomato bushes. 'Dennis gave me some a while ago. Never again! My bum's still burning.'

'Actually, my flatmate Len is learning to be a chef. He might like some for his cooking class,' I said.

Later on, Dennis handed me a little plastic bag filled with chillies. It reminded me of a bag of lollies.

'Remember what I said, Mick, they're strong,' he warned, as I stuffed the packet into my jeans pocket.

Later in the day, back in Fremantle, Nick dropped me off home after a bit of time spent propping up the bar at the Sail and Anchor. As I stood waving him goodbye, he suddenly dropped the clutch on his old Nissan Stanza and did a massive burnout on my driveway, just to embarrass me in front of the neighbours.

With the wheels screeching, Nick screamed off down the street, leaving me standing there in a cloud of thick smoke and my clothes smelling of burnt rubber.

I fumbled for my keys and wandered inside. Len and Chloe were out as usual. Then I fumbled for the light switch in the kitchen, helped myself to one of Chloe's home brews and plonked myself down at the kitchen table. There was a note from the landlord that said, 'Please clean the footprints off the walls in the hallway.' (That was where our phone was. Whenever any of us were talking on it, we would sit on the floor with our feet on the opposite wall.) 'The kitchen is a disgrace. Please clean the oven and the fat off the walls.'

I screwed the note up and threw it on the floor. Before I'd finished my beer, Len arrived home with his mate Gino.

A short time later, Len and his mate staggered in and joined me at the kitchen table for a beer. Gino was an alcoholic. He was only in his twenties and had a nice wife and young child, but every time he came round to visit, he was drunk. Luckily, though, he was a happy drunk.

We were all yakking away and getting a bit boisterous. One thing led to another, until Gino cried out, 'I've got the munchies. You blokes got anything to eat in this dump?'

I patted the pocket of my jeans. 'Hey, Gino,' I said, as I pulled out my little bag of chillies. 'Are you man or mouse, mate?'

I waved my little bag under his nose.

'Phoo! What do you mean, man or mouse, Mick? I love chillies,' he replied.

Dennis's warning was ringing in my ears: 'Only one chilli at a time, Mick.'

'Well, Gino, let's see what you're made of, buddy,' I said, egging him on.

'You bunch of fluffs. What are those piddly-arsed chillies going to do?' Gino said. 'Here, give them to me.' He snatched the bag out of my grip and poured a palmful of chillies into his hand.

I thought about warning him but decided against it. I watched him stuff the chillies into his mouth all at once. Then I sat there for a minute or two, staring in fascination to see what the outcome would be.

Well, we didn't have to wait long. Gino's facial expression changed about 50 times, like he was miming something. Then these unrecognisable sounds started coming out of his throat and he started making dry-retching, hocking sounds. Then he leaned over – 'Blugh, blugh!'

And I'll never forget it, ever. His face turned crimson and he broke into an instant sweat.

'I think I've killed him, Len,' I said, trying not to laugh.

Next minute, Gino bolted over to the fridge with a look of sheer terror in his eyes and started rummaging through it. He first tried swigging out of a milk container. Nah, no good – and threw it on the kitchen floor.

He dived back into the fridge and took a swig of cream. Nah, no good – he threw it over his shoulder.

Next, he opened a jar of pickles and scooped some out with his fingers. Nah, no good – he stuffed it back in the fridge.

In a panic, he started running around the kitchen like a chook with its head cut off.

By that time, Len and I were in hysterics watching poor Gino ramming his fingers down his throat, trying to chuck up – nah, no good.

He ran over to the sink and poked his head under the tap for a drink. 'You mongrels. You bunch of mongrels,' he said, in a hoarse whisper.

'Yep, he's coming right, Mick,' Len said, wiping away tears of laughter. 'He's abusing us. That's a good sign!'

Gino slowly came right about half an hour later. He saw the funny side of it and even asked for the rest of my little chillies to try out on his mates.

I was paranoid and I kept an eye on my food for days – I knew what Len was like.

10

The three amigos

I APPLIED FOR A job and got a start with an Italian crowd called Zipponi Earthmoving, which was owned by a little bloke called Enzo Zipponi. They had a fleet of diggers, mainly late-model Komatsus and a few Poclains, which were old dung boxes. Their main bread-and-butter contract was with the Water Authority of Western Australia. In the early nineties, the local government had decided to get rid of all the septic tanks that were slowly polluting the groundwater and leaching into the Swan River, so there were infill sewerage contracts all over the city.

Zipponi's was a really old-fashioned outfit, but it was well set up. They had a yard at Kewdale with a big workshop, but Enzo's office was in an old caravan, which he just about lived in.

Each week, on payday, we could choose between being paid by cheque, which we could pick up from Enzo's caravan in the yard on Friday (and wait a week for it to be cleared by the bank), or by cash, which was a bit of a drive out to the Zipponis' house in Wangara. There, Enzo's wife, Pandora, would hand out our pay packets in a little office built onto the side of their house.

It felt creepy when you walked in, because the office was always dark, with the blinds closed. Sitting behind the counter, beautifully dressed in a jacket with shiny sequins and dripping in jewellery, which sparkled in the light of a strategically placed lamp, was Pandora. She was an attractive, middle-aged Italian lady.

Each Friday, I would face 10 minutes of interrogation about what had happened on the site during the week, along with any juicy gossip Pandora wanted to share, before she would hand over my tiny pay-packet. After signing for it, I would breathe a sigh of relief as I grabbed the door handle and left the interrogation room, squinting my eyes as I made my way out and into the light of day.

The Water Authority ran gangs. Each gang had a leading hand or foreman, a head drainer and his offsider, one brickie, one chippie, a Franna crane hired from Brambles, an excavator hired from Zipponi's, a hired six-wheeler tip truck and Bobcat or a loader. These crews were a pretty multicultural lot. Most of the blokes were Italian and even though they'd been with the Water Authority for 20 or 30 years, they hadn't picked up English too well. I could only understand every third or so word, which I found a bit embarrassing to start with.

Early on, the drainer had to spend five minutes explaining something to me, of which only a quarter sunk in, then another five minutes during which maybe half had sunk in, then another five minutes ... until I said, 'Oh, got you! No worries.'

I learnt a lot from those blokes. They'd laid pipes for years and they knew all the tricks. Most of our work was in trench shields, down to about three or four metres deep. Most of Perth was built on sand, so the sites had to be dewatered before we could dig.

Because the city is so flat, all the grades for the sewer lines started off at the pump stations about 12 metres deep, then gradually rose to about three or four metres out in the suburbs.

My gang was run by a Belgian called Jan. He was a laid-back bloke and nothing fazed him. He had a battered, weather-beaten face from years in the hot WA sun and his skin was like leather. I joined his crew at Hamilton Hill, just south of Fremantle, where I drove a five-tonne Kubota excavator doing backyard hook-ups. This was great, as they were only about a metre and a half deep.

Working for the Water Authority, nothing was rushed. In fact, they made an art out of doing nothing. For example, one hot summer's day, we were all standing around in a group up the back of someone's property in the shade, when their big boss, Tony, pulled up in his white ute.

He hopped out of the ute, put his hard hat on and made a beeline for us. All the boys were panicking.

'We've been sprung,' someone gibbered.

Tony walked up to us with a stern look on his face. 'Okay, you blokes. I don't a-mind you standing around a-talking, but the public will ring up and a-dob us in,' he said, as he waved his hands expressively. 'So, stand in a-smaller groups. You two go over there behind-a that-a garage,' he said, and pointed. 'You two go and stand behind those-a bushes. You and Mick go and stand behind that-a firewood pile.'

So, yeah, there was a lot of wasted ratepayers' money.

In order to dig between two properties, we had to pull out all the fences on the boundary, and pretty much all of the fence panels were made of asbestos. There was no PPE in those days – we just had to dig down into the sand in front of the fence panels, then pull the sheets out of the ground and stack them. Once they were neatly stacked, we would dig the sewer line, then reinstate the soil and put the asbestos panels back into the ground. While this was going on, we were being bitten by thousands of pesky little ants or harassed by flies trying to crawl up our nostrils. The more we sweated, the more the flies loved us.

It was surprising what people who lived in Hamilton Hill grew in their backyards in those days. There were lots of naughty little cannabis plants growing between garages and boundary fences. I even saw one growing out of a hanging basket.

One day, old Joe, the drainer, turned to me and said, 'What a beautiful looking plant. What a-kind is it, Mick? Never seen one like that-a before.'

'You don't want that plant, Joe. It will get you into trouble and your kids will probably wind up smoking it.'

'What-a you mean?' He looked puzzled. 'I'm a-going to dig it up and put it in my garden beside-a my tomatoes,' he said, with a wave of his hands.

* * *

Back in the early nineties, some of the blokes at the Water Authority were pretty crooked. All the subcontractors had to buy one carton of beer a fortnight to give to the work crew. If you didn't supply a carton a fortnight, your work gang would find fault and boot you and your machine off the job.

I had to buy a carton of beer and pay for it myself, out of my wages, then wait a week to give Pandora the receipt. In return, she would reimburse me from petty cash. I wasn't happy about it because the wages weren't the greatest. Working five days one week, then four days the next week with Friday as my rostered day off, I barely made enough to live on. I even suggested to Pandora that they buy a pallet of beer and hand out a carton for us to give to them. She laughed at my idea.

While I was working there, I met up with Rod, a Bobcat operator who was also a subbie. He was your all-Australian bloke. We had the same sense of humour, so we became good friends. We used to carpool together, week about.

When his gang boss asked for his carton of beer one day, Rod replied: 'Bang it up your clacker, you bent bunch of jabberers. You've never even offered us one single can out of the box!'

'I'll-a make sure you're off this job if you don't,' the gang boss replied.

'Do what you like, Luigi. We've got a contract to supply a Bobcat. And if you don't like it, I can always ring up *The West Australian* newspaper and dob you in for corruption,' Rod answered back. Needless to say, Rob stayed with our gang.

The process of getting contractors and their machines on a job was pretty competitive, In order to get a contract, they had to tender at rock-bottom prices – and I don't know if it was true, but I heard all sorts of rumours about cash and free holidays sometimes being part of the deal.

Another sweetener was to throw two machines in for the price of one, such as a Bobcat and an excavator. Then it became an all-out war among contractors to undercut each other.

One morning, I arrived at work at a job at Shelley by the Canning River. Shelley was a desirable suburb in which to live and our gang was doing a sewer line there. I climbed up on the digger, a late model Komatsu 12-tonner, to check the oil. This wasn't because the machine used a lot of oil, but rather to make sure some shady character hadn't poured sand down the oil filler cap or into the hydraulic tank.

While I was there, I noticed the half-charred remains of a beer carton tucked down among my hydraulics hoses. Someone had obviously lit the carton, but the fire hadn't taken off. One of our excavators on another site wasn't so lucky and got burnt out. Another excavator was so badly graffitied and vandalised that it was carted away to get repainted.

Rod drove up to me in a cloud of dust in his Bobcat at lunchtime. 'Hey, Mick, have you seen that new zero tail swing Yanmar excavator Benito's got down that laneway over there? It's the first zero-swing five-tonner in WA apparently.'

'Oh, really? Let's go check it out and I'll grab a photo of it,' I replied. This was before the days of mobile phone cameras, so I grabbed my trusty old camera and followed him.

We wandered down the laneway and there was Benito digging away on his new five-tonner. He was an owner-driver. He stopped as we approached him.

'Gidday, Benito. Nice digger, mate,' I said. 'Mind if I take a photo of it?'

'You're just a-spying for Zipponi's. Mick, you take a photo and I'll-a throw your camera down in-a that-a trench,' he said.

I looked at Benito. 'Your digger is hardly top secret, mate. Throw-a that-a camera down-a in that-a trench, mate,' I mimicked, 'and you'll-a be-a following head first, straight after it, pal.'

That's how bad the rivalry between contractors had got – now the operators were copping it in the neck.

Our next job was building a new pump station over at Belmont. Jan was still our gang boss and we had a bloke called Pete as our drainer. Also on the crew were Steve, the chippie, and José, our alcoholic Spanish brickie.

When I started at the Water Authority, it came as a big surprise to me that we could drink beer or whatever else we liked at lunchtime. A lot of the old-school Italian blokes drank grappa, an Italian brandy with a very high alcohol content. I thought it was bad enough digging under a gas main sober, let alone pickled.

At Belmont, I was stripping some vegetation under a hedgerow one day when José the brickie came running out in front of my bucket.

'Stop, stop, Mick,' he shouted, waving his hands, before disappearing under the hedge.

I thought he'd spotted a boundary peg or something, but seconds later, he crawled back out carrying a six-pack of VB he'd stashed in the shade for later.

Another day, José was down about three metres benching out a manhole and having a beer as he worked. By about three in the afternoon, he was singing away in Spanish down at the bottom of his manhole, drunk as a skunk.

José climbed out of the manhole to make some more mud, which he shovelled into his bucket. He then staggered back over to his manhole and proceeded to lower his heavy bucketful of wet cement down the manhole on a rope, which got tangled around him in the descent.

He stumbled, then disappeared head first, straight down into the manhole, following the bucket.

'Crikey!' I yelled in horror as I jumped off the digger and raced over.

Jan, Steve and Pete casually walked over and peered down the manhole.

'Bloody José, drunk again,' Jan muttered.

'You reckon he's dead?' Steve asked, a look of horror on his face.

'Nah, he's snoring. He's okay. Let him sleep it off,' replied Jan. Then they wandered back to work.

On the Friday, we were laying big storage tanks, which were two-metre-round concrete pipes laid in four rows. There was only one pipe remaining to lay, which was left for Saturday – even though it was rare for us to work a Saturday. Laying the pipes involved my 22-tonne Komatsu digger pushing the pipe in, a Franna crane and Brambles' big crane – one to carry the pipe over and the other to lift the huge pipe into position.

The following morning, the big crane arrived and lifted the last tank segment in place. I pushed it into the collar of the last pipe. All done and dusted after only an hour.

'What's next, Jan?' I asked.

'We knock off, Mick.' he said.

'Knock off? What a waste of time.'

'Nah. Put eight hours on your docket book,' Jan replied. 'Didn't you hear? It's José's birthday. He lives just down the road and he's throwing a barbecue and beers.'

Jan gave eight hours to everyone, including Brambles' big, expensive crane and my digger hire. I thought it was criminal – all on the ratepayers again.

Later that morning, I was driving home and decided to call into Woolies and do my grocery shopping. I hopped out of the car and grabbed a shopping trolley. I never bothered to lock my old Ford Cortina back then.

When I'd finished my shopping, I wheeled my loaded-down trolley out to the station wagon, lifted the back door up in a daydream, placed all my shopping bags into the boot, took the trolley back to the trolley bay, then wandered over to the car and hopped in. I fumbled for my car keys and stuck the key in the ignition. But the key wouldn't turn. I wriggled it again. Still no luck. I sat there for some time, feeling like something wasn't quite right, but I couldn't put my finger on what.

Looking around the car, I noticed the blue upholstery. Blue upholstery? I was sure my car had red upholstery.

Wait! My car *does* have red upholstery. The penny dropped. I was in the wrong bloody car. I quickly jumped out of the car – all the while worrying that the owner might think I was trying to pinch it – then I grabbed my shopping bags from out of the boot and looked around desperately for my car. It was parked right next to the one I'd hopped into!

The owner of the other car must have thought theirs was an old clanger too, as neither of us had locked our car! He or she obviously had a sense of humour to park next to me, because both cars were identical on the outside.

* * *

One hot Friday afternoon I went to pick up my wages from Pandora at Morley. This day she was all dressed up, wearing a fine, deep-blue silk blouse and dripping with gold chains. She didn't scrub up too bad.

After my weekly interrogation, Pandora looked at me and said, 'We've hired a new employee, Mick, and we'd like you to be a mentor and show her the ropes about drainage. Her name is Lindy. She's come down from Kalgoorlie to operate one of our excavators. She has mining experience but hasn't had any infill sewerage experience.'

'Oh,' I replied. 'Show her the ropes? Yeah, no worries, Pandora.'

I exited Pandora's dungeon, thinking Lindy would be a bit of a rough diamond, given she was coming from Kal and was able to drive a digger. I'd never seen a woman digger driver before, so it was going to be a bit of a novelty.

Back out on the job at Belmont, we were all standing around in a group, yarning away, when suddenly an old Triumph Bonneville motorbike roared down the road before pulling up on site. The rider stepped off the bike and pulled it back on to its stand like a pro. Off came the helmet and all this long dark hair tumbled out. With a flick of her head, the rider wandered towards us to a chorus of 'Mamma mia!' 'Ciao, bella!' and 'She must-a be-a lost.'

'Gidday, I'm looking for Mick,' she said.

Feeling surprised, I replied, 'Hi, I'm Mick. You must be Lindy. How are you going?'

Well, she definitely wasn't a rough diamond. Lindy stood about six-foot tall, was slim and had a really cheeky smile. As I found out later, she could make a hard man blush and would give you a run for your money with her wit and naughty sense of humour.

Straightaway, she turned to old Joe and, grinning from ear to ear, said, 'I know what you're doing, you dirty old man. Stop staring at my bum. And you, too. Stop ogling my fun bags, ya bunch of old perverts!'

All I saw was a row of old blokes with red faces.

'I was not-a looking at your behind,' said Joe, with a wave of his hands.

'And we were not-a perving at your-a cleavage, honestly, Lindy,' said one of the others.

'Well, all right, I'll let you off this one time,' she said.

And so it began: Lindy had the whole crew eating out the palm of her hand. They treated her like royalty. The old boys would bring in jars of preserved tomatoes and fresh veggies from their gardens. It was as if they were paying homage to the lady of the manor.

She was even allowed to help out down in the trench. Back then, every member of the gang had an allocated job. The drainer would set the pipe and the drainer's offsider would pack around the pipe while all the other members of the gang just stood around watching them. When I first started with one of the gangs, I was told off for climbing down into the trench to lend a hand. 'Go back and sit on your digger, Mick. That's So-and-So's job,' I was told.

When my digging was done for the day, a loader or a Bobcat backfilled the trench while I reclined my seat and went to sleep or stood around and chatted to the boys. A tank of diesel lasted a week on the digger, so not much work was getting done.

A couple of weeks later, Rod and I headed out to Morley so I could pick up my pay packet. Rod pulled up to the kerb outside Pandora's house and we spotted a young bloke walking out of the office, looking a bit sheepish.

'Hey, isn't that Johnny who drives your new 30-tonner?' Rod asked.

'Yeah, that's him,' I replied, as I watched Johnny climb into his company Land Cruiser. Only a few of the boys had a company ute. Johnny drove off in a cloud of smoke without even acknowledging us.

'What a stuck-up prick,' Rod said. 'Not even a wave. Your lot are a cliquey bunch, Mick.'

'Tell me about it!' I replied.

Rod stayed in the car while I nipped inside to get my pay packet.

Pandora was dressed up in all her finery. In the dim light, I saw a big bunch of roses lying on the counter.

'Got a secret admirer, Pandora?' I asked.

'That's a gift from Johnny,' she replied. 'It was my birthday this week, you know.'

'Oh, happy birthday!'

'I also got a wonderful big box of chocolates from Paul,' she added.

Paul had just got a new 40-tonner and a work ute as well. I was starting to see a pattern forming here. What a bunch of crawlers.

By the time I got back to the car after my debrief with Pandora, I was in fits of laughter.

'What's so funny, Mick?' Rod asked.

'Well, Johnny's bought Pandora a big bunch of flowers and Paul's bought her a box of chocolates … all for her birthday, you know. Mmmm …' I said, while blowing kisses.

Rod laughed. 'What a pair of grovellers,'

The following Friday, I had some car troubles, so I arranged with Pandora that I'd pick up my wages on the Saturday. As I pulled up at the house, I noticed a young bloke mowing her lawns with a noisy Victa mower. It was Muzza, who drove Zipponi's new 22-tonner – and his work ute was parked out the front.

When Muzza saw me, he shot around the back of the house and that was the last I saw of him.

Rod just about wet himself when I rang him and described the latest member of Pandora's boys club. I named them the three amigos: Victa, Rosie and Chocolate Boy.

Back at Belmont pump station, things were ticking along nicely. Lindy and I got along well as we had the same sense of humour. We had a lot of time to stand around and chat, so we took the mickey out of the Water Authority frequently.

Lindy picked up drainage in no time and was soon digging away on her Komatsu 12-tonner. She looked a real laugh, wearing this metre-round Mexican sombrero while she worked. Her hat filled the cab and it looked like she had a giant lampshade on her head.

For a laugh, I borrowed her sombrero and jumped in my digger, and she took a photo of me.

The next day, Lindy was down in the trench and I was standing up the top, chatting to the rest of the boys.

'Hey, Mick,' she yelled.

'What?'

'You wearing red ones today?'

'Red ones? Red what?' I said, looking down at my shorts. 'Nah, Lindy, green shorts. You colour blind or something?'

'Nah, red ones. If you're going to stand up above me, I'm going to look up your leg. I'm only human, you know.'

'You pervert! What a pervert!' I said, in mock disgust.

The following day, I was in a daydream, standing up on the track of the digger as I fuelled it up, when out of the blue I felt an almighty tug on my shorts. The next thing I knew they were down around my ankles. Lindy had just dakked me!

I was trying to hold the fuel nozzle with one hand and pull my shorts up with the other, while Lindy was standing there, shrieking with laughter.

Eventually, something had to give and it was my pants. I gave up and let them drop back to the ground.

'Lindy, this is sexual harassment, you know. You can't go round dakking your workmates,' I said, trying to keep a straight face.

Then I heard Joe laughing. 'Hey, Mick, you've got a hairy arse, mate. Not a pretty sight!'

'Sick bunch of perverts,' I replied.

The next time I went to see Pandora, she looked very concerned. 'I've heard some disturbing rumours going around about you, Mick, from a reliable source,' she said.

'Rumours? What rumours, Pandora?'

'You know. It's about you and Lindy.'

'What about me and Lindy?'

'You're having an affair with her and she's already in a relationship,' Pandora said, with a knowing stare.

I cracked up laughing. 'You've got that wrong. She's going out with a big, hairy bikie, so there's no way I'd do that. Anyway, how did you hear that? I haven't spoken to anyone at

Zipponi's for months.' I wanted to add, 'They're all too busy mowing your lawns and buying you bunches of flowers and choccies,' but I didn't.

'Well, what's that photo of you wearing Lindy's sombrero in the digger? It's obvious to me that you're getting on pretty well,' Pandora retorted.

Then I clicked. Bloody Lindy! She'd got one over me again. She'd made up this bullshit story just to wind Pandora up for being so nosy. Classic!

11

Cheap entertainment at the pump station

THE WATER AUTHORITY SHUT down for the holidays about two weeks before Christmas, which meant, for once, all the Zipponi boys would be working together out at Armadale, digging out a big stormwater pond.

When I arrived out at Armadale, most of the other blokes had already been there for a week so they already had a system in place for digging out the pond. There were diggers everywhere, and Enzo Zipponi told me to hop in a PC400 and start pulling up the sides of the pond.

As I unlocked the 40-tonner, the three amigos appeared, wanting to know what I was doing.

'Just jumping into this 40-tonner,' I replied.

'No, you're not. Muzza's going to drive it,' said Chocolate Boy, while Rosie was grinning from ear to ear.

'I don't care what I operate. If it means that much to you

blokes, go for it,' I said, then hopped down from the digger and wandered over to one of the old Poclain excavators.

By lunchtime, some of the blokes were sitting under the trees in the shade. It was the first time I'd had the chance to have a yarn with them all year. Of course, the three amigos were there, chatting away, as I sat down. I quietly listened to their banter as I sat there trying not to upset anyone.

After a few minutes, Rosie got up and wandered off. Then Victa made his excuses and left and, finally, Chocolate Boy made his departure. I assumed they were going down to the local bakery to get some lunch.

When I wandered back to my digger, I saw the three amigos with a bunch of other blokes from the purple circle. I thought it was pretty rude.

There was only a week to go until the Christmas holidays, so I started to pull up the batters of the pond, not really knowing what was going on or what the proper levels were. Before long, Rosie walked over to me.

'This is my spot, Mick. Dig over there,' he said, pointing to a nasty, swampy area.

I'd just walked the digger over to my new spot when Victa started waving his arms around like he owned the joint. It was like being back at school again. Stuff this, I thought.

I got out of the digger, walked over to Enzo and said, 'I'll take an extra week off and start my Christmas holidays now, rather than put up with this rubbish.'

Enzo was fine with that.

The following Friday, instead of going to see Pandora at Morley, I had to go to the yard at Kewdale to pick up my holiday pay. I pulled up outside Enzo's caravan and parked beside a row of red work utes, then I banged on the caravan door and walked in. Enzo was sitting in the corner of his caravan having a beer ... with the three amigos.

'How you goin', Mick?' they chorused, each of them with a beer in his hand.

Just the sight of those three sitting there smugly having a beer and acting for all the world like we were best mates got my goat up.

'How's your lawn-mowing round, Muzza?' I asked. 'Still keeping Enzo's lawns nice and tidy?

'And what about you boys?' I added, turning to Rosie and Chocolate Boy. 'Got your flowers and choccies ready to give Pandora for Christmas?'

I was fizzing by this time. 'Crikey, Enzo, you've got to watch where you stand around here,' I said.

'Why?' he asked, taken aback.

'You might stand on someone's tongue,' I said.

Enzo burst out laughing.

Then I addressed the three amigos: 'If you blokes can't be civil or even speak to me during the year, don't bother with your pleasantries now, you bunch of hypocrites ...'

'Is that my pay packet?' I asked as I leaned over the table to help myself from Enzo's tray.

'Merry Christmas,' I said as I strolled out of the caravan.

* * *

After Christmas, I went back out to Belmont, where I was working with Gavin, who was one of Zipponi's operators. We got on well as he was a laid-back sort of a bloke.

Gavin had dug out most of the site works for the pump station with an old Poclain excavator, so obviously he hadn't been mowing Pandora's lawns. The whole site had to be dewatered before we could excavate for the pump station. In order to dewater the sandy ground, we sank spears, which were three- to four-metre-long plastic or metal tubes with a fine mesh metal filter on one end and a coupler on the other.

To get the spears into the ground, we used a six-metre hollow pole, which had a rubber hose attached to the top it. The hose was either connected to a fire hydrant or a pump that went to a big water tank.

The pole was bolted onto the bottom of the excavator bucket, which was extremely dangerous. I would raise the pole vertically with the digger and someone would turn on the water. Once the water gushed out of the bottom of the pole, I'd push it slowly into the sand and water would gurgle out of the ground.

When the pole was at full depth, I would pull it out quickly. I had to be careful that it didn't bend or flick out and possibly kill someone. It wasn't long before I decided enough was enough. Instead of attaching the pole to the bucket, I hung it off a chain, which was a lot safer, as it dangled but couldn't kick out.

Once the pole was back out of the ground, someone would quickly throw a spear down the hole.

We carried on boring holes and dropping spears down them until we had made a square pattern. Then the boys would go and couple-up all the hoses on top of the spears to a big plastic pipe that had connections all along it for the hoses. After this, they would connect the main hose at the end of the big pipe to a huge diesel-powered pump, which would suck the water out of the ground through the spears. It could take up to three days for the dewatering to be finished before we could begin digging.

Even then, we'd excavate the site down to three metres or so before we hit water again. Then we would go through the whole process with the spears all over again. This went on until we hit sandy clay at about seven or eight metres down. The dewatering spears are no good in sandy clay because the clay blocks up the filters so that the spears are unable to draw out water.

Instead, we needed to sink trench boxes in a square at the bottom of the pump station hole, then fill the boxes with blue metal to act as a sump. This enabled us to excavate down to the final level – which was easier said than done.

The ground at the bottom of the pump station had turned to slop, so Pete asked me to take my digger down into the bottom of the hole, where he wanted me to try to pull out all the trench boxes, as the sump idea had backfired on them.

My digger was a fairly light machine at 12 tonnes, so I took a gamble and dragged my way through the soft ground. It didn't feel too bad underneath all the slop. I managed to pull out most of the trench boxes on the far side without getting bogged down, but I knew I was pushing my luck. The longer I sat sit in one spot on soft ground, the more chance there was that I'd get stuck.

The vibration of the digger started turning the ground beneath it to jelly, so I admitted defeat, leaving just a couple of trench boxes in the far left-hand corner of the hole. I only just managed to drag my digger back up through the ooze onto hard ground. It was a close call and I knew I'd pushed my luck. Being bogged down in there would have been a real embarrassment.

When I got back to the site after my lunch break, Gav was in a bit of a pickle. He'd decided to take his digger down into the hole to get the last few trench boxes out and he hadn't been as fortunate as me when it came to getting himself out.

'So, Gav, tell me mate, in your wisdom, what made you go out in that slop?' I asked, staring down at the bogged Poclain excavator.

'Well, you went out in that slop, Mick, so, I thought, if you can I can ...' he said, sheepishly.

'Yeah, Gav, but my machine is 12-tonne and yours is 23. There's a slight weight difference, wouldn't you agree?'

'How are we going to get it out, Mick?'

'Well, first you'd better find a phone and ring your stepmother, Pandora, so she can ring your stepfather, Enzo,' I advised.

'Bugger off, Mick. She's not my stepmother.'

'Oh, I don't know, Gav. Her garden's looking well-weeded lately, mate.'

'Bugger off! I don't weed her garden,' Gav snapped.

I laughed. 'Well, I definitely know who mows her lawns.'

Eventually, Enzo turned up in his old XD Falcon. While he chewed Gav's ear off, I grabbed the spare Poclain from up on the stockpile.

While I was there, our serviceman Shano turned up. He was a stocky bloke with curly hair and always good for a laugh. He'd brought a set of chains with him to try to tow out Gav's digger.

Shano dragged the heavy chains down to the bottom of the hole and hooked them onto the towing eye of the track frame. At Enzo's direction, I started pulling away and, at one point, I nearly got Gav's digger out ... but it slid back down into the hole. The Poclain sank down on the other side of a trench box at the base of the ramp. This meant I had to try to pull Gav's digger up and over the trench box.

The back of Gav's tracks started slipping and sliding on top of the trench shield. Steel on steel is like a bar of soap. The more we mucked around moving Gav's digger, the more the ground turned to jelly with the vibrations.

Enzo booted Gav out and had a go on the digger himself. To break the suction, he tried to push with his dipper arm folded up. I could see what was going to happen.

Sure enough, the digger shot forward and sunk down on the folded-up dipper arm. He couldn't move the machine at all now. The whole weight of the digger was pushing down on the boom and dipper arm.

It was starting to get late by this time, so I suggested to Enzo that he get a heavy haulage recover truck with a 40- or 50-tonne winch. I had some experience with them and they worked well.

About an hour later, a heavy haulage truck arrived on site. The driver set up his winch rope through a block-and-tackle system.

The Poclain was about seven or eight metres down in the hole, and it was going to be a long, awkward pull on the winch rope to get it out. The driver was even concerned it might break his winch rope.

Reluctantly, he started winching. It was now my turn in the hot seat.

Bang! Something failed on the block-and-tackle pulleys, and the heavy haulage bloke was not a happy chappie. He decided he didn't want to do any more damage, so he called up a second truck, which arrived about an hour later.

By this time, it was about eight o'clock in the evening and dark. Being in the middle of a park in a residential area, there was quite a crowd gathering, with the locals taking turns at peering down into the hole. Even Pandora had turned up and set up a camp chair ready for the evening's entertainment.

Poor old Shano was dragging down a second winch rope, which he had slung over his shoulder, slowly pulling it down the steep slope.

'Oh, you he-man, you, Shano,' I called out, as he slowly passed me, pulling out his winch rope as he went.

'Yeah, Mick, I should be in the next Marlboro man advert. Give me a can of Solo when I hit the bottom, mate,' he yelled.

It was late in the evening, and the heavy haulage guys had set up their web of block-and-tackle pulleys.

I hopped back into the bogged digger and waited for Enzo's hand signals. The haulage trucks took up the strain of the wire ropes and started winching.

Bang! Something else broke in the dark and I slid back into the hole. This brought forth lots of naughty swear words and name calling from the heavy haulage drivers.

They decided to re-rig the block and tackle another way, but they made it very clear that if it failed again, they would leave because this job was causing too much damage to their gear.

I got back into the Poclain and the heavy haulage boys started winching.

Slowly, slowly, I crept up the side of the shoring box with my feet up on the excavator's front window to stop myself falling out of the seat.

Slowly, slowly, I could feel the suction releasing underneath the digger. I even managed to unfold the dipper arm and help push the digger backwards up the side of the trench box.

Slowly, slowly, the rear end of the digger came up until it was nearly vertical. At this point, I wished I'd put my seatbelt on, as my knees were starting to ache like anything and I was trying hard not to fall out the front window and embarrass myself.

Slowly, slowly, with one last push of the bucket, I felt the digger rock backwards, over the point of balance, and back onto hard ground again.

I could hear all the local crowd cheering above me and just make out their silhouettes in the glare of all the car headlights now parked in a semi-circle. It's just a bogged digger, I thought. Anyone would have thought think they were all at a local footie game – all the people clapping and cheering, and cars tooting their horns as their team scores some points.

I waved my watch in front of the dim light from the dashboard and I could just make out it was midnight, on the dot.

I climbed out of the digger, gave a bow and hobbled off to my car and headed home.

Western Australia's Kurara gold mine, Boomerang Pit, 1990, showing the exposed ore body in the high wall.

Ludlow Deviation on the Bussell Highway, South West region of WA. Aftermath of two dumpies trying to squeeze through a one-lane gateway at the same time.

A joy ride into Wiluna, one Sunday morning during the wet season.

Standing on the ore body in M1 Pit, Wiluna.

Just giving the ol' 984 a spruce-up one Sunday morning at Kurara.

Eon gold mine, Wiluna. This is what happens when you put a 44-gallon drum to one side on the back of a Hilux.

Start of shift, Southern Cross.
A row of 777s ready to head off.

Having a beer at Meekatharra while
waiting for our ride to Wiluna.

Skid Row, Eon camp, Wiluna.
Accommodation at its finest.

Dirk threatening to sack the lot
of us if the dozer is not out by 3
o'clock, M1 Pit, Wiluna.

Two D9Ls, one stuck in a sump hole during the wet season, M1 Pit, Wiluna.

'Caterpillar can opener'. A CAT 651E scraper buried inside a parked truck. Eon gold mine.

Kurara gold mine. Looking down at the boys hard at work in Boomerang Pit.

12
What's a levitation?

AFTER A YEAR AND a half, it was time for me to move on from Zipponi's. I'd got nowhere in the company and I had no intention of mowing Pandora's lawns in order to move up the ladder.

I scored a job with Eastville Contractors – a drainage company that mainly did subdivisions in Perth. They ran Kato excavators, which were good machines. I drove an HD1880, about a 43-tonner, that they used for boxing out the deeper trench lines.

The job paid better, but it didn't take long for me to work out that I just didn't like the company much. I knew I was hanging by a thread. One bloke, Stan, was a big Englishman, who sported a handlebar moustache and claimed he'd been in the RAF. He was a drainer's offsider in his mid- to late-fifties and he would have been a hard man in his time.

During the day, Stan was a screamer, then, at knock-off time, he tried to be best mates with everyone so he could cadge a ride home. All the boys would bolt out the gate so they didn't have to give him a lift. One afternoon, I got caught out.

'Hey, Mick, could you drop me off at home?' Stan asked, with a big, cheesy smile.

I thought he was two-faced, but my better nature prevailed. 'Yeah, okay, Stan. Jump in, mate. Where do you live?'

'Oh, just down the road, Mick. Not far.'

The pig – he didn't even take his dirty work boots off when he jumped into my nice clean car in his dirty clothes.

'Right, Mick, just turn down here,' he said, with a smile.

I turned off.

'That's good. Now, go down there.'

I kept driving.

'Keep going,' he said, about 10 minutes later.

After another 10 minutes he piped up: 'Now, just stop here, Mick.'

I pulled up outside a supermarket.

'I just need to nip in here for some fags, Mick,' he said, with the cheesiest of smiles as he bailed out the door.

About 20 minutes later he came out with his shopping. 'Sorry to keep you waiting, Mick,' he said, with another big smile.

He got in and we drove off again. 'Right, carry on down this road, then turn left.'

On and on we went. After a while, he said, 'Just pull up here, Mick.'

'Oh, is this where you live, Stan?'

'Nah, but since you're here I may as well go into the bottleshop and grab a carton,' he said, with a big, gushy smile.

The slippery sod was taking a lend of me.

Finally, we pulled up his driveway.

'Oh, thanks, Mick. You can pick me up at six, mate,' he said, giving me another beaming smile.

I had made my mind up about an hour and a half ago when we left site.

'Yeah, fine, Stan. Six o'clock it is,' I replied then gave him a big, gushy smile and a cheery wave goodbye as I drove off.

Early next morning, my alarm went off and I fumbled for the button to turn it off. Did I really want to work for those screaming skulls? Did I really want to pick up that cheesy clown? Nah, not really. I rolled over and went back to sleep.

* * *

I wasn't with Eastville for long, but my next job broke my record for the shortest time I'd ever worked for anyone.

I went for an interview with an earthmoving company in Perth. I walked into this bloke's office and he started firing all these questions at me. He sounded like a sergeant-major.

'Right, Mick, follow me,' he said, as he steamed out of his office and through the workshop, which was full of clapped-out CAT 631D scrapers, then popped out at the back of the yard, which looked like a graveyard for old machinery.

'Right, Mick, get on that Hitachi digger,' he ordered.

I wondered whether all the earthmoving crowds around Perth were full of tossers. I was nearly going to salute him. But I pulled my head in, as I needed the job.

'Right, Mick, what I want you to do is run your bucket over the top of the ground,' he said. He was trying me out and there was nothing wrong with that.

'Righto, Sarge,' I replied.

'What did you say?'

'Nothing, mate,' I called out over the drone of the digger's engine.

I revved up the digger, lifted the boom, swung my dipper arm out and started trimming the metal with my bucket.

'Stop, stop, stop!' he yelled in a booming voice, while waving his hands. 'I only want the bucket 50 millimetres above the ground. I don't want to see it touch the earth.'

'Right, 50 millimetres above the ground. Got that,' I muttered.

As I hovered the bucket slowly above the ground, the major suddenly dropped to his hands and knees and started peering under my bucket. Then he lay down flat on the ground to get a better view. I couldn't believe what I was seeing!

'Stop, stop, stop! That'll do,' he barked. 'Come with me, back into my office.'

He marched me back to his office and, before I could sit down, he said, 'Right, I've got a job over in Northbridge digging out contaminated ground for a new building site. I'm sending a 30-tonner over there in the morning. It's only a week's work. Do you want it?'

He was a complete tosser, but I figured I wouldn't have anything more to do with him after today, so I took the job and we sorted out the details.

When I arrived at Northbridge the following morning, I saw a Hitachi 30-tonner being unloaded off a float. There was a bloke standing next to it, who turned out to be Tom, the site foreman.

'Yeah, Mick, there's two big power cables running along there somewhere,' he indicated. 'Not too sure where, but your boss has the service drawings of the site. He should be here shortly.'

At that moment, a Kal Con ute pulled up. 'Bugger,' I muttered, 'It's the major.'

The sergeant major marched up to me and, with no introductions or pleasantries, not even a 'good morning', he pointed towards an old brick wall.

'Right, there's two power cables here somewhere,' he said.

'What size?' I asked.

'I don't know and it doesn't concern you,' he barked.

'It does if I dig them up, mate,' I replied. 'How deep are they?'

'It doesn't matter how deep. Just dig slowly,' he barked.

I was already getting cheesed off with this clown and the day had barely started. 'Doesn't it show you on the service drawings, mate?'

'I don't have the service drawings on me. They're back at the office,' he said.

'Well, it's all sand. I'll have a quick peep in the engine panels and see if there's a track spade tucked in there somewhere. If there is, I'll dig a pilot hole with that spade and, hopefully, find the power cables,' I replied.

As I pulled open a side panel on the digger, the sergeant major bellowed, 'It won't be in there. That's the radiator and battery box!'

'I know that, mate. But you can tuck a spade in there, and there's no harm in looking, is there, mate?'

I took a look around the other side and opened another panel.

'It won't be in there. That's the hydraulic tank,' he barked. 'Just get on your digger.'

I was quietly fizzing as I climbed up into the cab.

'Right, Mick, I want you to dig 300-millimetre levitations. No more, no less.'

I had no idea what a levitation was, but I felt like I'd give him a levitation in a minute. Keeping my cool, I called out: 'So you want me to dig off a 300-millimetre layer, mate? Is that right?'

'Yes, only a 300-millimetre levitation.'

'Okay, so if I dig this 300-millimetre levitation, as you call it, and we get down to, say, a 600-millimetre levitation or a 900-millimetre levitation, what's stopping the power cable being at a 500-millimetre levitation, or an 800-millimetre levitation?'

'Just get digging,' he barked.

I couldn't believe I was doing this: blindly digging for a power cable in sand and no shovel to find it with – and this clown wanted me to chop off 300 millimetres at a time. I shook my head.

It was too dangerous, so I decided to slowly whittle off 50 millimetres at a time. Doing it that way I had half a chance of not breaking the power cable. It didn't sit right with me.

'What are you doing?' roared the sergeant major – and Tom the builder was starting to look a bit uncomfortable, not knowing what to make of it – 'I said 300-millimetre levitations not 50-millimetre levitations!'

That was it. I slammed the digger off from full revs, which was not good for the turbo.

'Hey, mate, you can stick your 300-millimetre levitation right up your clacker. You will go down as the biggest tosser I've ever met. How did they hire you?' I asked, as I grabbed my Esky and drink bottle from behind the seat before wandering off to catch the train home.

That job lasted about half an hour.

* * *

I rang Ken at Kanny's and he told me to come and see him at 10 the next morning.

As I pulled up outside Kanny's yard the next day, I noticed they had moved up in the world, having been bought out by Macmahon, which was one of the biggest construction companies in WA. No more dark, dingy office full of big, hairy miners, but a new block of offices – well, probably second-hand, actually – in the form of portacabins stacked on concrete blocks out the front of their yard.

'Well, Ken, they really know how to look after you, mate,' I said as I gazed around his portacabin office. 'Does water run down the inside of your walls, mate, when it rains, like your dongas up in the bush do?'

'Umm, no, Mick, not that I know of,' he replied, before quickly changing the subject. 'I've got a position on a digger up at Lawlers, near Leinster. It's a good site.'

I took the job even though it meant leaving Perth.

A couple of days later, I caught the plane up to Leinster, which is about 900 kilometres north-east of Perth. A Toyota Coaster bus was at the airport to pick up a bunch of workers headed for the mine at Lawlers.

On the half-hour drive to the site, we passed through Agnew, which was once a gold-rush town but was now an old ghost town. There was an old headframe, stamp batteries and waste dumps that remained from those days, and only a pub still operating, as far as I could tell.

Further down the road, we pulled into Lawlers Gold Mine camp. The camp was built beside what had been the goldmining town of Lawlers in the late 1800s. The town, which had had a population of over 8,000 souls in its heyday, was long gone.

Once I got sorted out with my room key, I wandered along a red-dust-stained footpath, taking note of where the wet mess and dining room were. It was another typical mining camp – nothing flash.

I walked past rows of red-stained dongas and a few dying, scrubby plants scattered about the camp. I saw the tail of a bungarra sticking out from under a donga. It must have been having a snooze among the beer-bottle tops and smoke butts littering the ground underneath the dongas. I saw the usual 'day shift' and 'night shift' signs hanging off the door handles of the dongas, and I heard the clanging sound of clothes dryers as I walked past the laundry room. I took note of where the public phone booth was before I headed to the camp store later to buy a phone card. Yep, it was as depressing as I'd expected.

The landscape around the camp was flat and scrubby in every direction. The scrub was littered with old tin cans, broken glass and pieces of rusting corrugated iron from the old township.

At my donga, I sat on the end of the bed with my head in my hands. Here we go again. Another six weeks to go.

I always got an empty, lonely feeling, almost like being homesick, when I started in those places. I didn't know anyone. I wondered whether my dirt boss would be a screamer.

I got up and decided to go over to the dining room for a feed.

While I was sitting by myself, having dinner, two blokes covered in red dust plonked themselves at my table.

'You new here, mate?' one of them asked.

'Yeah, fresh off the plane,' I replied.

'Well, I'm Jezza, the head shotfirer, and this is my offsider, Scottie,' he said. 'You probably won't understand much of what he says ... he's Scottish!'

'Bugger off,' muttered Scottie.

'Quiet, haggis breath, I'm talking,' said Jezza, with a grin. 'What have they got you doing up here, mate?'

I introduced myself and told them I was a digger operator.

'Well, Mick, I wish they would hire us some more blokes. We're struggling at the moment on the shot crew. There's only me and Scottie, and he's not much use!'

The pair of them were a real laugh and we hit it off straight away. I'd never worked on a shot crew blowing things up. It sounded interesting.

'Hey, Jezza, would I be able to jump the fence and work with you blokes? Wouldn't mind trying something different.'

'Yep, I reckon I can make it happen,' he replied, and – true to his word – he did.

The following morning, I jumped into the bomb ute, which was a Toyota Land Cruiser with big explosives signs on the front and back, and we headed out to the magazine. This was the first time since I was 17 that I wasn't going to be driving a machine for work.

Over the next few weeks, Scottie showed me the ropes. I couldn't get over the fact that I was standing there with my stemming stick in my hand, watching all these stressed blokes doing the work I was usually doing. There were dump trucks driving back and forth, production diggers chipping and scraping and dozer drivers pushing off the waste dump. I grinned to myself.

We worked three pits: Hell-Purgatory (or HP Pit, as it was called, because we weren't allowed to say Hell-Purgatory), Caroline Pit, which was between HP Pit and the camp, where they were doing a cutback widening the pit from the top, and New Holland, the furthest pit, was down the road near Agnew. One of my jobs was to load holes with explosives, mainly ammonium nitrate fuel oil (ANFO), basically fertiliser with diesel mixed through it. The drill holes were about 75 millimetres wide and drilled to a depth of five metres.

First, we would mark out a drill pattern with a spray can. The drill pattern was marked out in a grid pattern. The dots were sprayed out in rows, about two metres apart. Then we'd move over and start another line, aligning the dots between those in the previous row. We could end up with 20 or 30 rows, depending on the blast area. If we marked them out properly, we could eye along your lines diagonally and the dots should all be in straight lines. They were fairly strict on this.

If the ground got harder, we might change the size of the drill pattern, moving the rows closer together, marking the drill holes one-and-a-half metres apart. If we were marking a drill pattern up beside the high wall of the pit, we would mark out pre-split holes along the high wall. They would be drilled at the same angle as the high wall, say, 65 degrees.

Once the drill pattern was marked out, our Ingersoll-Rand drill rigs would move in and one of the drillers, Bam or Trev, would start hammering away. If the drill pattern wasn't finished, night shift would take over. We were always hot on their heels, waiting for the drillers to finish the pattern, and we would sometimes start loading the blast holes while they were finishing off their drill holes.

To load a blast hole, we first connected a Nonel, which is a thin plastic tube about five metres long with a detonator crimped on one end and a plastic clip on the other. We would then poke the detonator end through a booster, which is a small cylinder filled with high explosive. We needed the booster to initiate ANFO as it is a low-sensitivity explosive. Next, we fed the booster connected to the Nonel down to the bottom of the drill hole.

We would place a rock on the plastic clip temporarily, to stop it from falling down the hole, then we carried on dropping boosters down all the drill holes. After that, we would load up the drill holes with ANFO pellets, known as prills. On a big shot, we would use a vacuum truck to do this.

The truck would drive along the rows of drill holes and dump a specified amount of ANFO down each hole, which saved us heaps of time.

Once the drill holes were loaded, we would each grab a stemming stick – like a long, oversized broomstick handle – which we used, along with our boots, to tamp dirt down into each of the holes. This repetitive process eventually chewed the heck out of my knee joints.

With the drill holes backfilled, we rolled out the detonator cord along each row and cut it, leaving a short tag end that would be joined onto the plastic Nonel clips sticking out of each drill hole. Once all the Nonels had been clipped onto the det cord, we tied delays onto the ends of the cord between each row. A delay looks like a dog's bone with a detonator in the middle and clips on each end. We used 25-millisecond delays between each row, so once the fuse was lit, we would hear a loud bang-bang-bang as each row blew up. That gave the explosive enough time to blow up the rock in each row and push the rock forward to allow the next row to blow up and push forward, or heave, as we called it, over the face.

Once the delays had been tied in, we had to be careful where we walked. If any of us stood on or accidentally tripped over a delay, it could explode, setting the whole lot off.

Once the delays were tied on, the shot was treated as live.

Near the end of shift, Jezza would crimp his det onto the safety fuse, using his pliers behind his back to prevent him from losing his family jewels if he over-crimped the det and it went off. He would then tape the detonator onto the det cord.

All the mining machines would be parked out of the way. Blast guards would be placed along all roads leading to and around the pit. Jezza would then call up on the two-way radio: 'All blast guards in position.'

One at a time, we would all respond: 'All clear'.

Jezza would turn the siren on in the bomb ute as he headed down into the pit. There, he would light the fuse and jump back in the ute.

'Fuse is lit. Fuse is lit,' he would call over the radio as he rattled his way out of the pit.

Meanwhile, the dirt boss, Fruitjuice they called him, would be at the top of the pit, looking out for rifling blast holes with their tell-tale signs of smoke rings floating up into the air.

If a hole rifled, it hadn't been stemmed properly. It would then leave a pinnacle of solid rock behind that a poor old digger driver would have to scratch around or a dozer driver would have to rip it.

Once the blasts were finished, Jezza would head down into the pit to check for any for misfires. Meanwhile, the blast guards would wait until we got the all-clear from him before racing back to the wettie as the dust settled over the pit.

Over in New Holland Pit one day, Jezza, Scottie and I had just tied in the delays and were standing having a breather and admiring our handiwork with our backs to the high wall when we heard a tinging noise as a rock rolled down onto our 'Danger Explosives' sign.

We all turned around at once and saw part of the high wall slowly, silently moving towards us as a slip came down.

Jezza started running towards the shot area, yelling, 'Cut the bloody delays, boys, or we'll all be dead.'

So, we had a marathon delay-cutting session while constantly looking over our shoulders, shitting ourselves. As I cut off the last delay, I turned around to find the slip had stopped right behind my foot.

'Poo, what's that smell? Did you crap your pants, Scottie?' Jezza asked, laughing.

'Bugger off, Jezza. At least my face isn't as white as a ghost!' Scottie retorted.

'Mick, you're not saying much. You're not snorting something you shouldn't be, mate?' Scottie asked.

'Dream on, haggis breath. I don't need to do drugs – I get a natural high from life,' I said, while winking and blowing Scottie a kiss.

'You're a sick bastard, Mick,' he said, and grinned.

Slips and explosions weren't the only hazards we faced. I was walking over an area we had blasted the day before in one of the pits, and I noticed what looked like white fibreglass chunks all over the pit floor.

I picked up a chunk and turned to Scottie. 'This looks like asbestos,' I said, breaking a piece off and peering closely at it. 'I've seen pictures of it before.'

'Yeah, it is. But it's white asbestos, which I've heard is okay for your health.'

I cringe thinking back to those days when Jezza would light a fuse, let off a blast then pull his shirt over his nose and disappear into the dust haze to check over the blast for any misfired holes.

13
Bottom of the food chain

WHEN JEZZA GOT PROMOTED to supervisor, a new shotfirer
called Bert was hired. He was a tall, bearded, good-natured
bloke, who helped me out a lot with my never-ending questions
on shotfiring, as I was studying for my shotfirer's ticket in the
evenings for something to do.

One afternoon out on the shot, we loaded the blast holes
right up to the drill rig, which was over in the corner of the
pit, and were just finishing off a couple of drill holes. The rig
was cut off from tramming back out, the plan being that, once
he was done, the drill rig would straddle one row of loaded
drill holes and drive out. This was slightly unorthodox, but
common practice.

Then who should turn up unannounced but a mines
inspector – and he pinged us. Once the inspector had gone,
Fruitjuice came down to the shot and said quite a few
unpleasantries and swearwords, accompanied by lots of finger
pointing at Bert.

Next thing, I was driven back to the workshop to pick up the old CAT 769A water cart, which I filled up then raced back to the shot area.

As I backed up to the loaded shot holes, Jezza was there but Bert had disappeared. Jezza grabbed the big rubber hose off the back of the water cart. I turned on the pump and revved the old water cart so he could flush out the loaded shotholes. Once that was done, we pulled out the Nonel cord and booster.

We went six metres wide each side of the water cart and flushed out all the holes until we reached the drill rig in the corner. Then the blame game started.

Later, I was called into Fruitjuice's office and he wasn't a happy chappie. 'I've just tramped Bert. What's your excuse, Mick? Give me one good reason why I shouldn't sack you,' he roared. 'What were you bloody thinking?'

It was clear that this had turned into a major butt-covering exercise for Fruitjuice. 'I don't have any excuse, mate. Just following instructions,' I replied.

'Instructions!' he roared. 'You should know better than that.'

'Well, you fellas taught me. I thought that was the norm. You blokes have done that since day one,' I said. He knew it and I knew it.

'Right, I'll give you one more chance, Mick, and that's all. Now get out,' he roared for the last time.

I wandered out of Fruitjuice's office thinking that if he sacked anymore blokes, he'd have to get the office lady and the cleaner to start loading shot. Us powder monkeys were at the bottom of the food chain, so nothing would have surprised me.

After that episode, Scottie got brassed off and snatched it. Jezza went back to supervising. While Fruitjuice was waiting for a new shotfirer to arrive, I wound up loading and tying-in by myself. Once I'd done all the work, Fruitjuice would turn up, light the fuse and take the glory – unless he felt generous and let me light the fuse.

On my next break back in Perth, I'd booked to sit the exam for my shotfirer's ticket. These exams only took place a few times a year, so I hit up Fruitjuice for a note to say I had done my time so I could sit it. He wouldn't do it, the miserable sod, as he reckoned I was one month short of my time – even though I'd spent two weeks loading shot and tying it in by myself anyway, and letting a blast go.

When I got back from my R & R, I'd canned the idea of sitting for my shotfirer's ticket for the time being. The days were starting to warm up and the flies were getting friendlier, so I decided it was time to get back in the air-con again.

As luck would have it, an old ute pulled up on the shot, and a lean, haggard, long-haired bloke climbed out. Gee, he looks like Sam, I thought.

'Gidday, Mick, how've you been? What on earth are you doing stemming holes out in this heat? You gone troppo or something?' he asked. It was indeed my old mate.

'How you going, Sam? Where have you been hiding?'

'Not at Her Majesty's pleasure, if that's what you're thinking. I'm your new leading hand,' he said.

'Oh, good. That means you can pull a few strings then!'

He laughed. 'I've already pulled them. Jump in, Mick, I've got a little job for you.'

We rattled off in the old Land Cruiser over to the Caroline Pit.

'We've started a cutback, over on the far side,' he said. 'Hop in that digger and start pulling those batters and I'll spot you with my clino,' he said.

A clino or clinometer is about the size of a matchbox and is used to measure the degree of a slope. You put the clino to your eye and peer through a little sight glass as you look down the slope.

After I cut the slots all around the pit walls, Sammy left me to pull the batters. Battering is probably the hardest thing to do on a digger, so it takes a good eye. It was funny watching the dump truck drivers going back and forth, peering out at me and taking a second look.

Halfway through, Todd, one of the dump truck drivers, called me up. 'Hey, Mick, didn't know you could drive a digger,' he said.

I replied, 'Never driven a digger in my life, mate. Easy, aren't they? Don't know what all the fuss is about.'

'Yeah, right,' he said, and laughed.

Then everyone got on the two-way and gave me a ribbing.

A bit later, Fruitjuice came screaming up beside my CAT 245 digger. He called up. 'I want to talk to you!'

'Shit, that doesn't sound too good,' I muttered, wondering if I wasn't supposed to be operating the digger.

'Mick, you bastard, I'm spewing about you,' he said, with a grin.

'Why? Have I stuffed up your batters?'

'No,' he replied. 'For not bloody telling me you're an all-rounder!'

That was how I rose from the bottom of the food chain to the top in one day – but I still drank with the boys no matter what job they did.

* * *

Sam and I were sitting outside his donga having a beer one evening, when this slim, blonde chick walked past.

'Who's she, Sam?'

'She's just come over from the other shift: a dumpy driver. Don't go there, Mick, if that's what you're thinking. Stay clear of that one.'

'What? You got your eye on her, mate, have you?'

'Nah, nah. Nothing like that. Just warning you. Her name's Lexie, but they call her the Doctor.'

'The Doctor?'

'Yep. The Doctor because you can get any pill you want off her.'

Sam wasn't wrong – it turned out she was pretty much running an illegal chemist shop from her donga and it wouldn't have surprised me if Sam had been one of her customers.

One day, I was driving the CAT 769A water cart, which was a laugh to drive. It had three gears and would rear up when you changed gears and billow out black smoke as it laboured uphill. You would stick it in first, drive off till a red buzzer light came on, pull the lever into second gear – the front would rear up and cause the water in the back to surge – keep accelerating till the red buzzer light came back on, pull the lever into third – she would rear up the front again – and away you'd go. If you hit a steep incline, like the base of the waste dump, the old girl really reared up and threaten to flip over backwards, especially if the water cart was full.

We were backfilling part of the old cyanide tailings dam, which involved tipping the waste rock over the side and down into the poisonous slop below. I had just finished a run on the haul road leading up to the waste dump when I passed Todd in his dump truck, gave him the fingers and got a rude gesture back. I noticed the Doctor was tipping beside one of Lawlers' white utes, which had its door open. The ute was reversed back to the edge of the waste dump with its tailgate down – nothing unusual, as everybody used the waste dump as a rubbish dump. The shot crew would throw away the big silver bags that the Nonels came in and the Anfo bags went over the side as well.

At the end of shift all the dump trucks would park up in a straight row on the Go line. Then we would pile into the Coaster bus and head back to camp, looking forward to a nice cold beer.

Back at camp, I wandered over to the wet mess to buy a carton of Emu Export. When I walked through the door, there was a near riot going on.

'Where's that clown, Craig? Why hasn't he opened up the bar yet? This is bullshit,' someone muttered.

'Sack him,' someone whinged.

'Who's got the keys to open up this joint?' someone else called out.

Craig was the barman in the wet mess, and he'd got his job through Fruitjuice, possibly because they were related. He acted as if he owned the joint. If he didn't like you, he would leave you standing at the bar for ages. He'd even kick people out for having dirty clothes, which was ridiculous given where we worked. He was just the wrong guy for the job.

Next minute, the Doctor was standing beside me, puffing on a ciggie, one shifty eye on me and the other shifty eye roaming the room. A bit like 'one eye on the pot and the other up the chimney'. You didn't really know which eye to look at when talking to her.

'Hey, Mick,' she said. 'I wish Craig would hurry up. I saw him up on the waste dump throwing rubbish down the face, off the back of his ute, at about two o'clock. It was a pain in the neck having to tip our loads off beside his ute all afternoon. He even left his door open, the dickhead. I hope his ute is full of dust.'

'Come to think of it, I noticed a ute up there about five o'clock, but no one was in it,' I said. 'Was it still there at knock-off time?'

'Yep. It must be broken down or something. Bit strange, leaving it there,' she replied.

'I'm going to bloody snatch it if this caper keeps going on. A bloke can't even buy a beer in this joint,' some big, hairy miner whinged beside me.

Norm, one of the leading hands, wandered in. 'Where's Mr Personality?' he asked.

'Don't know,' the Doctor answered. 'But his ute's been up on the waste dump all afternoon with the door open,' she added matter-of-factly.

'On the waste dump? Shit, that sounds a bit strange. I'll go for a drive up there and have a look around,' said Norm.

A while later, Norm strolled in, waving the keys for the bar. Suddenly there was a chorus of cheers and mutterings of 'About time.'

A scruffy fitter yelled out, 'You're a bloody legend, Norm. I was starting to dry out, mate.'

Once the bar was open, Norm told me what had happened: 'Just as well I went up there, Mick. I pulled up to Craig's ute and was having a look around when I hear this faint cry. So, I have a peep over the side, and down below in the slope is Craig, white as a sheet and shaking like a leaf, buried up to his waist in mud. Of course, I took compassion on him. I yelled, "Where's your bloody keys to the wettie, cobber? This is no time for a mud bath – there's a near-on riot back at camp."

'You should have seen him, Mick. His eyes were as wide as saucers, he had a look of sheer terror on his face, and he reckoned he'd broken his leg. If he wasn't such a tosser, Mick, I would have felt sorry for the poor bloke. He was a mental wreck. Imagine, triple-sevens and triple-seven-threes tipping all afternoon over the edge right beside him and his ute – and huge rocks sailing over the face, rolling down around his ears. Stuff that! He was bloody lucky.'

It turned out Craig had been standing on his tailgate throwing the rubbish off the back when he tripped and went down with it.

We never saw Craig again. He upped and left that night.

14

Pride of the fleet

THE FIRST TIME I drove a dump truck was at Lawlers. Their training programme was pretty straightforward: 'Hey, Mick,' said Norm. 'Jump in with Lexie, mate, and she'll show you the ropes.'

I was quite excited as I climbed up the ladder into the cab. I sat in the little dickey seat beside the Doctor, then off we went down into HP Pit to get loaded.

Once the digger driver had thrown a load on the back then tooted his air horn, we started grinding slowly up, out of the pit towards the waste dump, picking up speed as we went.

Next minute, there was a call over the two-way radio from Norm, who was following right behind us: 'Yeah, just pull up here, Lexie.'

The Doctor pulled over to the side, grabbed her gear and opened her door. She was smirking.

I was puzzled. 'Where're you going?'

'See you later, Mick. I'm off to catch the plane for my R & R. You'll be right!' she replied as she disappeared down the ladder.

That was my training for Kanny's on how to drive a dump truck: half a lap in the dickey seat, then jump behind the wheel and work the rest out for yourself. Mind you, it wasn't exactly rocket science.

Speaking of a rocket, we had a spare 50-tonne dump truck, which was a clapped-out piece of junk. It continually billowed out black smoke as it was driven down the haul road, so you could see it coming a mile away. Even so, it went like the clappers, out-pulling the other dump trucks at the pit, so we nicknamed it 'the Rocket'. When I was driving it, no one could pass me in a drag back down into the pit, which we weren't meant to do anyway.

The truck had no rubber flap on top of its big mudguards, which meant red mud would splatter off the big tyres and onto the wing mirrors as it was driven down the wet haul road. When it came time to reverse the truck under the digger bucket, I could barely see the digger in my wing mirror. But I had it sussed. If you could see a little spot in the mud-splattered mirror and actually see the digger bucket while you were reversing, it still didn't matter, because the mirror vibrated so badly that you couldn't see the digger anyway. That said, it was a hoot to drive.

We only really used the Rocket as a fill in. When the digger was loading out ore, it was a longer haul, so instead of using three trucks we would add a fourth truck into the circuit so as not to keep the digger waiting. One of my jobs was to cart ore for an hour or two when required.

On a mine you get all sorts of digger operators. Some are good blokes and some are prima donnas. Kanny's new digger driver, Danno, was the latter. He'd pick on the poor dump truck driver and make his life a misery by making him pull out and reverse back in again, or he'd overload the dump truck big time, so that the load went from the back of the tray right over to the front above the cab, leaving a big mound, or haystack, or ice cream, or whatever you want to call it.

Mind you, if I was on the digger, I'd sometimes haystack my mates on the last load of the day, for a laugh, then I'd give them a toot, a cheery wave and a nice smile. They'd be none the wiser until they went to tip their load off, which sometimes they couldn't do, so they'd have to throw their load off instead.

This involved pulling the dump truck forward and reversing as fast as you could back to the tip face. Just as your back tyres hit the windrow at speed, you had to slam on the retarder and brake while lifting the tray lever down beside your seat at the same time. The dump truck would then rear up at the front and the motor would labour and groan. While the truck was still rocking on its suspension, the dump tray slowly started lifting off the chassis, inch by inch, gaining momentum until, finally, the hoist managed to tip the load off. If you stuffed the timing up, you'd pull forward, grit your teeth and do it again and hope you don't mess up and wind up over the edge.

'Copy, Mick,' came a voice over the two-way.

'Yeah, Norm.'

'Park that digger up, mate, and jump on the Rocket for a few rounds till that ore's dug out.'

I made sure my five-litre drink bottle was full then climbed up into the Rocket and took off in a cloud of smoke down into HP Pit where Danno was digging.

All the truckies laughed at me as I threw a cup of water on the Rocket's mud-splattered wing mirror then grabbed the mirror arm to stop it vibrating so I could see the digger while I reversed back under the bucket.

So far, so good – Danno hadn't had a whinge at me yet – but I was waiting. He had only been on the job for a few days but already you could hear him on the two-way radio, ranting and raving.

After about an hour, the transmission on the Rocket started to get hot, which meant it had a mind of its own. If I stopped completely and selected 'reverse', it would hesitate and sit there for a minute or two before it decided it wanted to go into reverse. However, for some strange reason, if I put it into reverse while it was still rolling forward and about to stop, it would clunk into reverse. It was just a matter of timing.

Anyway, I got down into the pit and, as I rolled forward slowly – clunk! – the Rocket went into reverse. I fired a cup of water at the mirror, quickly rubbed a small circle clean so I could see, and grabbed the vibrating mirror arm – all while idling back slowly. Then I planted my foot and flew back towards the digger bucket.

On the next round, we were in a tight area that only had room for one truck at a time. Todd passed me. Now it was now my turn. I slowly rolled forward to whack the Rocket in reverse, but I stuffed up the timing and rolled forward into the high wall with a bump and abruptly came to a halt.

Bugger!

As I sat and waited for reverse to kick in, I heard Danno's voice over the radio: 'Come on, mate, I haven't got all day!'

'Yeah, just a minute, Danno,' I replied, laughing.

'Can't you drive that bloody thing, mate? You're holding me up,' he spewed.

'Yeah, sorry. It's got a mind of its own,' I replied. By this time, I was in hysterics as I looked out the window to see the other dump trucks starting to queue up.

'Bugger this bullshit. I can't wait all day for you, pal,' shouted Danno. 'Will one of you other truckies use your noggin and back up under my bucket?'

'Can't,' replied the Doctor. 'Mick's blocked us off.'

As I banged the dump tray up and down on the chassis to try to jar it into gear, Danno roared, 'Would you hurry up, pal?'

I grabbed the radio: 'How about you just shut your trap, buddy?'

The other dump truck drivers were laughing their heads off and giving me the thumbs up. I knew how Danno was thinking – something along the lines of: What dump truck driver would have the audacity to answer me back?

'What did you say?' Danno yelled through the airwaves.

Norm's voice cut in over the two-way: 'Just bloody have patience, Danno. We know we have issues with that dump truck.'

Clunk! The Rocket suddenly shifted into gear, so I backed up quickly, without time to clean my mirror.

Danno tooted his air horn. 'No, pal,' he ranted. 'Pull out and move over a foot or so.'

'Just load me, you meathead, or you'll be waiting another half hour for the truck to find reverse,' I replied.

Norm interrupted us once again: 'Just do what Mick bloody said, Danno, and shut up.' I liked Norm. He was old school.

The following day, I was playing around on an old 988B loader, pushing up sheeting material over the back of HP Pit when Norm pulled up in a cloud of dust.

'Jump in, Mick. Got a job for you down the pit after smoko, mate,' he said.

We rattled our way down into HP Pit, where I gave Norm a hand with the hot-water urn and foam drinking cups, then I pulled out a box of wine biscuits as the dump trucks pulled up one by one for smoko.

Just before the end of smoko, Norm called me and Danno over.

'Right, Mick, you're loading trucks for a couple of days until we get a new digger driver.' He turned to Danno: 'Jump in the wagon, mate, you're sacked for banging that Lawlers bloke's head on the window of the bus last night.'

There was no mucking around in those days.

Danno walked around to everyone, shaking their hand, but totally ignored me as he climbed into Norm's old wagon.

15

A soak in the sump and a walk in the bush

'I'VE GOT A JOB for you on the loader, Mick,' said Sammy one morning. 'Out at the borrow pit loading out a few loads of sheeting material.'

We drove in Sammy's old ute to HP Pit, where the loader was parked. He patted his pocket and pulled out an old tobacco tin.

'You into rollies now?' I asked.

'Nah, Mick, just going to have a quick choof to start the day.' He casually started packing his little pipe – made of brass fittings by the look of it – and lit it up.

'Look out no one catches you, mate,' I said.

'Nah, the trucks won't be here for another half hour,' he coughed.

In the afternoon, I had to take the loader out to New Holland Pit, which was a few kilometres down the road. To get there, we used to sneak down a private haul road, which Leightons used to cart ore along, with their big Kenworth off-highway trucks.

About halfway along the haul road, I spotted Sammy discreetly parked under a gnarly old gumtree, puffing away on his pipe. Neither of us were meant to be using the road, so I kept on going.

When I got to the other end of New Holland Pit, I pulled over and waited for Sam. Quarter of an hour later, I spied a red-dust cloud coming towards me.

Sammy pulled over and wound down his window. 'Okay, Mick, they want a ramp put in over there,' he said, pointing towards a cutback they had started. 'It's just for the shot crew and explosives truck. It's almost knock-off time, Mick, so give me a hoy when you're done. We'll leave the loader here tonight and I'll come and grab you at six o'clock,' he said.

At the end of the day, I called Sammy as instructed.

'Okay, Mick. I'll be there shortly. Could you go over to Murray on the drill rig and let him know I'll pick him up as well? His radio must be buggered. I can't get hold of him.'

'Yeah, copy that,' I replied. I walked over to Murray's drill rig, which was parked on top of the cutback area right beside the edge of the old pit. His door was open and his drill rig was still running, so he couldn't have been far away. Then something caught my eye and I started laughing. Murray was sitting in the sump hole right below me. He was up to his shoulders in water, having a soak.

I stopped laughing when I realised he was fully clothed with a backpack on. Why would anyone wear a backpack in the water?

I looked a little closer and could see that the top of the backpack was open. It looked like it was full of rocks.

I rubbed my eyes and muttered, 'I must be seeing things.'

Maybe Murray had visited the Doctor and taken something he shouldn't have and was counting UFOs in technicolour. I didn't know what to make of it.

When Sam pulled up on the drill pattern, he asked where Murray was.

'Umm, he's just having a quick dip down in the sump hole with a pack full of rocks,' I replied, thinking this place was a madhouse.

'What are you dribbling on about, Mick? Where's Murray?' Sam asked again.

'Come and have a dorrie yourself, Sam. I think he's tripping or something. You'd know more about that than me,' I said, and grinned.

'Oh shit,' he muttered. 'I'd better call Fruitjuice. Tell you what, Mick, you take the loader back and I'll sort this out.'

Back at camp, I was sitting on my doorstep having a beer and chatting to Todd. Next minute Fruitjuice came round the corner with the camp manager. 'You blokes haven't seen

Murray, have you?' he asked, looking rather concerned. 'We're trying to find him.'

'Nah, mate,' I replied.

After a while, Sammy came over to give me an update. 'Fruitjuice is in the shit. He sacked Murray after fishing him out of the sump.'

'Was his pack full of rocks?' I asked. 'It looked like it.'

'Yep, but it gets worse. The night-shift driller hopped into Murray's drill rig to fill out the pre-start card, then noticed a whole pile of heavy-duty suicide notes written on the back of the pre-start cards. Fruitjuice is crapping himself.'

Being a typical dirt boss, he had ranted at Murray, calling him a fruit loop, nutter, dickhead and every name under the sun, then dumped him off at New Holland's smoko shed and told him to get lost and catch the night-shift bus back to camp.

An hour later, Fruitjuice received a call from the night-shift supervisor informing him of the suicide notes, so he rang the Leinster police, who immediately asked if he'd tried to keep Murray calm and reassure him, and whether he'd kept an eye on him in the meantime.

Fruitjuice didn't have a leg to stand on. He could hardly say, 'Nah, but I hauled him out of the sump, sacked the clown and called him a fruit loop and a nutter, and told him to get lost.'

So, yeah, Fruitjuice didn't handle the situation too well.

Murray still hadn't been found by the next morning. What got the authorities worried was that he hadn't taken his wallet, which they found left in his donga. By then it had become a search and rescue operation and the police took over.

They first shut down the pit operation at Western Mining, as some of the staff were trained in search and rescue methods. But they had no luck locating Murray.

It was the third day of the search and rescue effort and they hadn't shut us down yet, to my disappointment. We were boarding the bus when I spotted a police trail bike search and rescue team out the front car park area of our camp, getting ready to head off into the bush. They looked the part in their trail bike helmets and gear. On the fourth day, I think it was, New Holland Pit was shut down, and, to our annoyance, we weren't picked to help with the search. The search and rescue blokes had a turn at wandering round in the scrub, but to no avail.

By that time, there was a helicopter in the air looking for Murray, as well as a light aircraft. The search even made the news on TV.

At the end of the week, instead of hopping on our Coaster bus to go to work, we were mustered into a meeting room at the camp, where we were greeted by a policewoman who was clearly expecting.

'Morning everyone,' she said. 'We have decided to shut your mining operation down for today and we will be forming a search pattern for the deceased.'

'Murray, you mean?' I called out.

'Yes. We're now looking for a body. If any of you find it, I don't want anyone to touch it or move it. It might be hanging from a tree.'

I piped up, 'Murray won't have much luck trying to hang himself out there. It's all bloody scrub about four-foot tall.'

Everyone started laughing.

The officer gave me the look – you know, the one you get when your old man's about to boot you up the backside. She continued: 'It may be lying down a mineshaft, so make sure you look down any old shafts, but be careful of the edges.'

'I suppose he'll be smelling like a dead kangaroo by now,' I piped up.

'Okay, what's your name?' the officer asked.

'Mick.'

'Put out your hand, Mick. I've got a present for you, since you're a bit of a livewire.'

I reluctantly put my hand out, thinking she was probably going to handcuff me, but instead she placed a roll of pink flagging tape into my hand.

'What's this for?'

'Well, you've got the job of flagging around the body,' she replied, and smiled.

'Oh, good one. Now I have to flag off a stiff that's been cooking out there for days.'

Everyone was laughing and patting me on the back: 'Good on ya, Mick.'

The lady police officer carried on and drew a picture on the board of how far apart to stand from the next person so we could still call out to each other.

We all filled up our five-litre drink bottles, slapped on heaps of sunscreen and Aeroguard, then hopped on the bus, eager to be on our way. Our search area was going to be out the back of New Holland Pit because that was the last place anyone saw Murray.

We piled off the bus and formed rows about 20 metres apart, then we headed towards an old waste dump on the horizon that we would use as our bearing so we wouldn't get lost.

It all started off properly: everyone was taking the search seriously, combing the ground and peeking into nooks and crannies. By 10 o'clock, it was starting to heat up, and by 12 o'clock, it was stinking hot and in the forties. The flies had woken up and were swarming over our sweaty backs and attacking our eyes.

Suddenly, the Doctor screamed.

Shit! My heart started pounding. She's found him, I thought.

We all came running over. 'What is it, Lexie?' I asked.

'That, that lizard,' she stuttered, 'poked its tongue at me.'

She had just about stood on a huge bungarra. We all stared down at the bungarra, which was minding its own business, basking on a flat rock, and we broke out laughing.

I breathed a sigh of relief and carried on searching.

By one o'clock, the novelty had worn off and tempers had risen.

'Shit, if I find him alive, I'll throw him back down the mineshaft,' one of the dump truck drivers said, after tripping over and falling down one himself.

Then Todd yelled out, 'Hey, Mick, come and have a look at this down here.'

An icy wave of dread ran down my spine.

'What is it?' I asked, as I reluctantly peered down the old mineshaft he was standing inside.

'Look at this cool old bottle,' he said, holding it up in his grubby hands.

I breathed a sigh of relief for the second time.

Some of the other blokes had come over and were peering down at Todd.

'Hey, that's cool. Bugger looking for Murray,' someone muttered.

Boys will be boys, so we gave up looking for Murray and went fossicking for old bottles and old mining memorabilia.

Our search finally ended at the old waste dump that was on the horizon when we first started searching. There was no sign of Murray.

As we hopped over an old fence on to another mining lease, we spotted a bloke on a Chamberlain tractor crane. He looked at us, puzzled.

'Gidday, mate,' Todd said. 'You haven't seen a stiff lying round here, have you? We're looking for one.'

'No, but six men have died down there,' the bloke replied, pointing to an old pit. That's Emu Pit,' he said quietly.

'Look, sorry man,' Todd replied. 'We didn't realise. Sorry, no disrespect, mate.'

'No, it's okay. I heard about that bloke who's gone missing,' he said.

It turned out that Murray had been hiding out in an old mineshaft close in beside New Holland Pit, and at night time he'd snuck back into New Holland's crib hut, which was well stocked with pies and sausage rolls in the freezer, grabbed some food and bottles of water then snuck back out into the bush. Eventually, he decided to leave and stuck his thumb out on the road back to Sandstone. That's when he got recognised by a truckie who had seen his face on TV.

His little jaunt would have cost hundreds of thousands of dollars with the shutting down of several mines, not to mention the planes and helicopters in the air and the search and rescue teams.

* * *

Early one morning, I woke up to the sound of a woman screaming and yelling, 'Get your filthy hands off me, you mongrels. Don't touch me!'

Then I heard men's voices and someone said, 'Come along, you're under arrest. There's no point resisting.'

I poked my head out of my donga door just in time to see the Doctor being unceremoniously dragged off by the police. That was the last I saw of her.

After work that night, I saw Sam sitting outside his donga having a beer with some of his mates. I hardly ever saw Sam after work, as he would normally disappear with his mates somewhere discreet.

As I walked up to them, they went quiet all of a sudden and looked at me.

'Giddy, Sammy,' I said as I pulled up a plastic chair beside him.

They had faces on them like someone had just died. After a moment, they carried on talking.

Sam piped up, 'If we catch who dobbed in the Doctor, look out!'

'Yeah, we know people who will do something about it,' one of his hairy mates said, eyeing me suspiciously.

'We'll give him a walloping when we find him,' said Sammy, looking at me intently.

'What are you staring at me for, Sam?' I asked. 'Do you think I dobbed her in or something?' I glared at him. 'I've known you for years, mate, and the stuff you take, I could have dobbed you in years ago, if I was going to.'

'I was just saying, Mick, that's all,' he said, somewhat mollified.

'Well, have you considered it was more likely a room cleaner who stumbled on her drug stash?' I asked.

Sammy and his mates were hacked off, having just lost their supply chain. They were probably also sweating it in case the Doctor dobbed them in as well.

* * *

One October afternoon, Fruitjuice picked me up at the airport when I flew in from my R & R break. 'Gidday, Mick,' he greeted me. 'How many beers've you had?'

I thought that was a funny question to ask. 'Oh, about four or five,' I replied.

'That's good, Mick. You'll be going straight on to night shift. Throw on your work clobber and we'll head out to the mine. You're on a dump truck till Christmas.'

It was a long night. The crew was so short-staffed, Fruitjuice was on a digger and he even put the office lady on a dump truck.

A lot of blokes left the mines in the run-up to Christmas so they could take off to the beach over summer and spend all their money. Most companies struggled to keep what staff they still had by the time Christmas itself came around.

I had done three months straight without a break when Christmas came around. It was the usual scenario. 'Mick, you have to stay working over the Christmas break,' Fruitjuice said to me.

'Sorry, I can't, mate, I've got family that have just flown over from New Zealand to see me,' I replied.

'Sorry, can't help it, Mick. You will have to stay,' he said firmly.

'Well, you let that new chick on the dumpie go on break,' I protested. 'She's only been here three weeks.' I was thinking to myself she must have fluttered her eyelashes at him and he'd let her go.

I shook my head and said: 'Sorry, mate, I've already done 12 weeks. Any longer, and that's just taking the mickey. My family comes first, so I'm going.'

And that was that.

16

The Belgian

EARLY IN 1994, I moved from Perth down to Bunbury, which is about 170 kilometres south of Perth. It ticked all the boxes: the climate was cooler and the fishing great. There, I got a job working for East Bunbury Civil.

Calum, the boss, ran a couple of Komatsu 22-tonne diggers and a couple of old CAT dozers – a D6D and an old D6C direct-drive swampy. John was one of their other digger drivers. We worked together all around the South West region of WA, building dams and ponds and doing major roading jobs. We also worked in the mineral-sand mines, so we had plenty of variety.

From time to time, we worked at a mineral-sand mine called Jangardup, a couple of hours' south of Bunbury, down past Nannup. The mines manager there would save about three days' worth of jobs then call us.

It was strange to see a sand dredge floating on the natural water table in the middle of a farmer's paddock, or a dredge pond as it was called. Minerals would be separated in a wet concentrator that floated behind the dredge. The sand and fine tailings would then be fired into the air and returned to the dredge pond. Eventually, the tailings would all get rehabilitated back to pastureland, and new fences and drains would be put in. It looked to me like the farmers got their land back in better condition than when they started. All their old, swampy paddocks drained much better after the coffee-rock layer under the ground had been chewed out by the dredge.

At Jangardup, Cable Sands were mining for ilmenite, which is the main source of the titanium dioxide used in paints, inks, plastics and even cosmetics. Once the ilmenite was processed and placed in a big stockpile, road trains would cart it back to Bunbury. It looked like sparkly black sand but, man, was it heavy.

Les, the mine manager, took me around the site and pointed out what work he wanted done. 'Right, Mick, first job. See that sandy point sticking out about ten metres into the dredge pond? Could you go out there and dig down about a metre below the water level so our pontoons linked to the dredge can float over the top without catching? Remember to leave your door open on the digger, just in case!' he warned.

I walked my 22-tonne digger out on to the point, left my door open and – just to be on the safe side – I opened the sun roof as well.

I started digging the layers of sand and soft coffee rock down to about a metre below the water. I couldn't see exactly how deep the dredge pond was because it was a deep chocolate colour but it looked eerie and sinister when I peered down into it.

A dredge works like a giant underwater vacuum cleaner. The cutter head does a big arc from one side of the pond to the other, chewing at the face while the sand gets sucked up into a pipe at the same time.

After I'd been digging away merrily for about half an hour, I scooped up another bucketful of sand and threw it behind me. As I slewed back to take another scoop, all I saw was dark, chocolate-coloured water lapping quarter of the way up the digger and the front of my tracks sticking out in mid-air. My sand peninsula had oozed away into the eerie depths of the dredge pond, nearly followed by me, so, I walked the digger back slowly and gave that job a miss.

About a month later, Calum dropped off our two excavators on the side of the road at Capel, which is about 30 kilometres south of Bunbury. The state government had invested a lot of money into upgrading the road from Perth to Bunbury and Busselton. When we started work at Capel, the four-and-a-half kilometre road bypassing the town had just been finished by Barclay Mowlem. However, the state's roading department had knocked back some of the bypass, saying that the shoulders on the dual carriageway were too wide. John and I were hired to redo all the batters and open drains down the length of the bypass. This meant sitting on rubber conveyor belts, so as not to chew up the new bitumen, in one lane, as cars and trucks flew past behind us, showering the diggers with chip metal off the new road as they went. It took us almost three months to finish the job, but it was satisfying work.

Just as we were finishing our work at Capel, Macmahon started work on the next stage of the new highway, the Ludlow deviation, which skirted around the town of the same name. It included 16 kilometres of new road and three new river bridges. We were in the right place at the right time, so we moved from working on one bit of the road to another.

The boss running the show was a Belgian known to everyone on the project as 'van Sackem' because if you didn't perform, he would boot you straight off the job. He was a slim man of average height, probably in his late forties. He was quietly spoken as a rule, but he had a way of speaking to you as if you weren't the full quid. He made sure everyone hated him, as he reckoned it gave better productivity.

A new haul road was going to be built on a causeway over a swamp to the base of a hill, which was to be our borrow pit. The plan was to dig sand out of the hill and cart it back to the highway. Everyone had a turn digging in the borrow pit. It was hit and miss where you dug. There were pockets of slime left over from the mining days, which made it hard for the six 773B and three Volvo 25-tonne dump trucks and they kept getting bogged in it. Macmahon started using dump trucks when the haul got longer.

Halfway along the causeway was an old farm gate, which we pulled off, although we had to leave in the big strainer posts for the farmer. This meant our dump trucks had to give way to each other at the gateway.

There were high-voltage power lines hanging low across the haul road, so, when we loaded the trucks, we had to be careful that the load was level with the top of the dump tray that went over the cab, otherwise the load would clip the power lines.

I had just finished loading a dump truck, and, as it went off in a cloud of black smoke, I sat and watched it head down onto the causeway. Then I spotted an empty 773 coming back along the causeway to pick up a load.

There was plenty of room for the dumpies to pass each other on the causeway, but, as they converged near the gateway, neither of the drivers looked like they were going to slow down.

They got closer and closer. It looked like they were playing chicken with each other. Closer and closer they came. Then there was a loud bang as the two 773s hit each other, head-on.

The empty truck flew over the side of the causeway while the other truck had its right-front wheel, strut and all, torn off. It also left its fuel tank behind on the haul road as it flew over to the other side of the road, where it ended up buried nose-deep in the swamp.

Surprisingly, both drivers walked away unharmed. But we all knew what the Belgian would have to say to them.

I walked my digger down to the crash site and scraped the load off the truck that was leaning into the swamp on a precarious angle, ready to tip over. We tried pulling it out with a D6 dozer, but it wouldn't budge. It sat there for a week while quietly getting plundered for parts by the fitters.

At the end of the week, a D9N dozer arrived from a mine site down the road. The dozer driver managed to skull-drag the dump truck out of the swamp. Then he towed it unceremoniously down the haul road to a spot where it could be winched onto a float ready to be taken away the next day. The poor old dump truck even got plundered out on the roadside for parts that night by the locals. By the time the tow truck arrived in the morning to pick it up, it was minus the batteries and air-con compressor.

As this was a long, spread-out job, we had to walk the diggers for kilometres down the new formation to do bits and pieces, such as digging out swamps or ripping out tree trunks and strip for borrow pits. I learnt one thing about walking the digger for kilometres at a time: they don't like it. The track rollers would heat up on a hot day and blow out their seals with a loud bang, then the stink of burning oil would hit you. If you let the roller flop around on the undercarriage too long, it would disintegrate and fall off.

I had to undercut the width of the road for half a kilometre, the reason being that the area had been mined for mineral sand in the fifties and sixties and the old slimes ponds left behind were full of wet clay that had been backfilled with sand. The slimes were just as sloppy as the day they'd been put back in the ground when the area was first mined.

As I was digging out one of the ponds, I got down to three or four metres and still it was slop. I tried to stockpile the slimes, but they just oozed all over the ground.

Soon, van Sackem pulled up in his Hilux, then Bill, the main road inspector for the job, pulled up in his ute.

When van Sackem walked over and looked at the hole. 'We can't build a road over that, Bill,' he said.

'Yes, you can, Van,' the road inspector replied.

'No, you damn well can't,' roared van Sackem, then he turned towards me and said, 'Mick, stick your fingers in your ears for a moment please.'

'Bill, come over here. Like I said, I can't build a road over that slop,' the Belgian barked.

'I want you to stop digging and put the slimes back into that hole,' Bill yelled.

'But you can't even stand on that slop,' van Sackem yelled back.

'I don't care. Just do what I tell you, Van!'

Eventually, they came to a compromise and Bidim cloth was rolled over the hole, then it was bridged with about a metre-and-a-half of sand – and it worked.

My next job was to dig out the sand from under a bridge after the bridge deck had been craned onto its piles. There was a bloke on a Bobcat working next to me and, as usual, van Sackem was sitting in his ute parked up on a hill, keeping an eye on everyone.

Next minute, van Sackem came screaming down the hill, heading towards us. I didn't know if it was me or the Bobcat driver he was about to tune up, so I was relieved when I saw him veering left towards the other bloke. He climbed out of his ute and walked over to the Bobcat. Here we go, I thought.

I stopped the digger and climbed out of the cab to read what was written on one of the cut pegs, but I was able to hear van Sackem as clear as a bell.

'What's your name?' he asked the Bobcat driver quietly.

'Tom.'

'Well, Tom,' said van Sackem, 'could you move your Bobcat over to the side a little bit?'

Tom complied.

'Yes, yes, Tom. A little more. A little more. Yep, that's great,' van Sackem said, in his steely, expressionless voice.

'Why do you want me to park her?' Tom asked, still sitting in his Bobcat, looking puzzled.

'Okay, Tom, now could you please turn your engine off.'

Tom turned the engine off.

'Great, thank you, Tom.'

Tom started to climb out of his Bobcat.

'No, no, you just sit there please, Tom.'

'But what for?' asked Tom.

Van Sackem's face turned crimson and he roared, 'So your bloody boss can come and pick you up. You're sacked.'

This was all par for the course for the Belgian. I was just glad that it wasn't me on the receiving end of it.

One morning, I was battering the sand around a bridge abutment and had hopped out to read the level on the peg, which was on top of the abutment. As usual, van Sackem was watching.

He climbed out of his ute and came over to ask me what was wrong.

'Your bloody surveyor's getting all technical on me,' I replied. 'The peg says, "cut two to one-and-a-half".'

Van Sackem walked over to the peg, read it, shook his head, gave the peg a good wriggle then ripped it out of the ground and threw it in the creek.

'Okay, Mick, just make my abutment look pretty,' he said, then he walked off.

By lunchtime, I'd nearly finished the batters around the abutments, ready for Bill to inspect. A couple of young blokes, who were doing a bit of labouring down below the bridge, started walking up and down the batters of the bridge abutment that I'd just tidied up, and they left footprints everywhere.

When van Sackem pulled up in his ute ready to meet the roads inspector, he noticed the footprints and quietly asked who had made them.

'Those two clowns down there, I said, nodding in the direction of the labourers.

Van Sackem looked down at the bridge, pointed to the young fellas and waved at them to climb up the batters.

A couple of minutes later, they arrived huffing and puffing to where the Belgian and I were standing. It was a hot summer's day, about 35 degrees.

'Okay, boys, so you like climbing?' van Sackem asked, with a smirk.

They looked at each other, none the wiser.

'Okay, boys, do you have any landscaping experience?' van Sackem asked frostily.

'Oh, yeah, a bit,' one of them replied.

'That's good. Do you boys know how to use a rake?'

'I do,' the other one replied.

'Well, that's good,' van Sackem roared. 'You two can bloody go round all the abutments and rake out all your footprints, and if it isn't done by the time I get back, I'll sack the pair of you!'

A few days later, van Sackem picked me up in his ute to show me a couple of jobs. We pulled up on top of a hill. He started explaining a job he wanted done, then he stopped in mid-sentence: 'Why has that dump truck stopped?' He pointed. 'Why is that bloke on the water cart talking to the dump truck driver?' His voice was slowly rising. 'Why is that digger sitting there with its bucket in the air and no truck underneath him?'

By this time, we were rattling down the hill, heading straight for the unfortunate dump truck driver, who was yakking to his mate.

Van Sackem turned to me with a look of glee. 'You know the old story, Mick: a new broom always sweeps clean,' and he sacked the dump truck driver on the spot.

Me and the Belgian used to have some ding-dong rows, but he never sacked me. He was good at his job, keeping production going. He just didn't suffer fools.

One morning, van Sackem was in one of his sarcastic moods as he pulled up beside me in his ute.

'Copy, Mick,' he said over the two-way radio.

'Yeah, Van,' I answered.

'Right, Mick, see over the back of the borrow pit. I want you to strip off some more topsoil by that pile of logs.'

'Yeah, okay, I'll make my way around there.'

'Well, personally I would cut across the floor.'

'Nah, there's an old slime pond down there.'

'So what? It will have dried up by now. Just cut across there, like I said, and stop pussyfooting around.'

'Nah, I'm not doing it. I'll go around,' I said.

'You'll do what I tell you,' he barked over the two-way.

I looked down at him from the digger and called back to him on the radio, 'Hey, Van, read my bloody lips!' I slid back the driver's door window and poked my head out, mouthing an obscenity. 'Got that?' I asked, mouthing it a second time. I was fizzing.

He looked at me with a smirk and drove off.

* * *

Van wasn't the only who got sworn at on that job. I copped my fair share of bad language too and, on the odd occasion, I probably deserved it. On one of those occasions, I was eating lunch in my digger at the bottom of a creek bed. Beside me was a big stockpile of sand I had dug out of the creek. The front window of the digger was pinned up and my feet were hanging out the quarter window when a farmer rode up to the edge of the creek.

'Hey, mate, I wouldn't stay down there too long,' he said. 'Bloody tiger snakes will have a go at you. Happened to me the other day when I was fixing the water pump over there.' He pointed at a pipe coming out of the creek bed.

'Thanks for the warning me, mate, I'll keep an eye out,' I replied, then went back to munching on my sandwich and listening to the radio.

Then, out the corner of my eye, I saw something move between the stockpile and the digger. I peered out the right-hand window to get a better look but saw nothing. When I turned to look back out the front, there was a huge tiger snake slithering over the top of my track just below my hanging feet.

Oh shit! My knees shot back, nearly landing behind my ears. The snake just stared at me.

'Woah, woah, don't you come in here,' I said, still holding my knees behind my ears.

The tiger snake poked its head over the glass, had one more look at me, turned and slithered off down the track, heading straight towards a couple of surveyors, who had their backs to it.

Now, one of these surveyors was not very popular with the boys. I started to laugh. Should I warn them?

Nah! I waited a bit longer and watched the tiger snake getting closer and closer to them.

When the tiger snake was right behind them, I called up: 'Copy, survey. Copy, survey.'

'Yeah, copy,' one of the surveyors replied.

'Do you blokes like snakes?' I asked.

'What are you on about, Mick?' he replied.

'Better look behind you ...'

'Ah, crikey!' he cried, as they both bolted for cover.

A bit later, a shaky voice came over the radio: 'Mick, you tosser, you could have warned us sooner!'

'Yeah, sorry, mate, I only just noticed it,' I said.

Between the snakes and the Belgian, work out on the roading project was pretty hard going, and John and I did some big hours for our boss, Calum, with little thanks. At Christmas time, we drove to his yard next to his house for a shout. When we got there, Calum pulled two beers out of the fridge, which for the most part of the year had been sitting on the floor of his corrugated-iron workshop. To make things worse, it was a brand of beer neither of us used to drink. Luckily, we had thought to bring our own beers.

Calum's lack of generosity didn't sit too well with John. After one too many beers and a few too many puffs on a naughty smoke, he went after Calum, who managed to lock himself inside his house.

After lots of naughty swearwords outside Calum's window, which echoed all around his lifestyle block, John staggered back to the workshop and plonked himself down on a chair.

'Crikey, Mick, we do over 80 hours a week and this is the best he can do,' he said.

'Yep, he's a miser alright,' I agreed. 'Come on, John, let's drive back to Bunbury and find a pub to celebrate Christmas.'

17

Till the next teardrop falls

AFTER THE LUDLOW DEVIATION job, John went back down to Jangardup and drowned his 22-tonne digger out on a tailings dam. He broke through the crust of the dam then sank down flush with the exhaust pipe. Mind, you it wasn't hard to drown a digger on that site. The mines manager tried it on me as well, but I put my foot down and said, 'Bugger off, I'm not doing it.'

Poor John had a run of bad luck. On his way home from Jangardup, he hit a roo but didn't stop to check for damage. The roo had gone underneath his ute and broken the plastic bung on the bottom of the radiator, cooking his motor.

Meanwhile, I had just finished building a dam on a bloke's farm at Dardanup, just out of Bunbury. I parked the digger in some long grass on the side of the road for Calum to come and pick up.

I dug out the mud and rocks from my tracks so they couldn't bounce off and break a car window while the digger was being floated down the highway.

It was a stinking hot day and I was dressed in my usual shorts and tee shirt. The flies were particularly bad that year. As I was standing in the long grass, shovelling mud and rocks out of the digger tracks and sweating like a pig, the flies were swarming all over and around me, attacking my eyes and trying to crawl into my ears. I could feel them tickling my legs.

'Bloody flies,' I muttered as I brushed my legs without even looking down.

'Damn pesky little sods,' I muttered as I brushed my legs again.

Still muttering, I swiped my legs again. They felt like they had dozens of flies swarming over them.

'What on earth's going on down there?' I muttered as I walked out of the grass and into the open.

I looked down and my legs looked like something from a horror movie. They were teeming with five-centimetre-long bull ants. I'd been bitten by a bull ant on the toe once and it was painful.

I stomped around in circles, in sheer terror, yelling, 'Ooh, ow, ow, ow.' Then I stomped down the dusty gravel road, yelling, 'You ugly little sods. Get off me,' doing my best war dance impersonation until the last ones fell off.

The strange thing was, I never got bitten once, but I made a mental note never to dig tracks out in long grass ever again.

After that, I headed down to Bridgetown to widen a dam for a future vineyard. Calum came down with the D6C swampy to give me a hand. He was a good dozer driver.

Calum always wore jet fighter pilot shades – you know – the teardrop 'Aviator' Ray Bans with the dark green tint. Well, they didn't suit him, but he thought they looked cool.

I had just sat down on a log for lunch and was pouring a cup of tea out of my Thermos when Calum wandered over and leaned against an old jarrah tree. He was looking dapper, dressed in his tight denim jeans, thumbs hooked in his belt loops and, of course, the dark teardrop fighter pilot Ray Ban shades, projecting the epitome of coolness. But unfortunately, he had one major flaw which he didn't seem to notice.

I took one more look to make sure, then, having tried to hold back for as long as I could, I burst out laughing.

When Calum started laughing, I went into hysterics and couldn't stop.

He abruptly stopped laughing. 'What's so funny, Mick?'

I looked up at his face. 'I think you're missing something, Calum,' I said as tears of laughter streamed down my cheeks.

I took one last look at Calum's teardrop fighter pilot shades, but it was hard to have an intellectual conversation and keep a straight face with a bloke standing there, thumbs hooked in the tops of his skin-tight jeans, looking the epitome of coolness, with one lens missing from his sunglasses. The other lens was on the ground.

* * *

My next job for East Bunbury Civil was just out of Balingup, a place well-known as home to people from all walks of life. I arrived at the lifestyle block and found my digger parked up a long, gravel driveway. The property was set back into the side of a rocky hill surrounded by jarrah forest. The owner, Ken, was a down-to-earth bloke who was a sparky by trade. He wanted me to deepen a pond on the side of the hill behind his house, so that if a bushfire came raging through, he could activate a pump up at the pond that would set off some sprinklers on his roof and hopefully save the house.

The house was situated right beside a rocky bluff, no doubt for the views. Ken reasoned that when it rained in winter, the water would cascade over the bluff and flow down into the gully. He certainly lived in a beautiful part of the South West.

When the job was finished, I walked the digger down the driveway, which Ken shared with his neighbours. Just as I was locking the door on the digger, a sky-blue Volkswagen Kombi van with yellow flowers painted on it pulled up beside me.

Inside the van was a nice-looking chick and a long-haired bloke. When the girl climbed out, I noticed she was dressed like a hippy. She walked towards me over the rough, hot, gravelly driveway in bare feet and she didn't even flinch.

'Hi, man. How you doing? I'm Jane. Sorry to bother you, man,' she said.

'Nah, it's okay,' I replied. 'What can I do for you, Jane?'

'Well, we saw your big digger, man, and we just, like, wondered if you were interested, man ...' Her voice tapered off.

I took one look at her face and it was clear that she was high on something very naughty that's blue and sprouts up in the bush once a year around those parts – so high, in fact, that she was almost hovering above the ground.

'Well, man,' she said, 'our driveway needs fixing. Would you be interested in, like, giving us a quote on how much it will cost? Look, we can't pay you cash, man, but I can give you something worth your while.'

Now, I don't know if she meant she meant sex or magic mushrooms as payment – I wasn't a hundred per cent clear on that one, so to make her happy, I said I'd have a peep on my way out.

'Far out, man, that'd be absolutely kaleidoscopic, man,' she said.

Now, I don't know whether that was the spectrum she was viewing me through at that moment, but she turned and hovered back to her Kombi van and they drove off in a cloud of dust.

I stood there, muttering, 'Kaleido-what? Never heard that one before.'

Then I just jumped in my ute and kept going, straight home. If I'd gone up to their place, I probably wouldn't have been able to find my way home for a week or two afterwards.

* * *

Macmahon had won a contract down at the new Beenup mineral-sand mine near Augusta, and they rang Calum and asked for a digger and dozer.

John and me were sent down together. Depending on which way you travelled, it was nearly a two-hour drive one way from Bunbury.

Most of the contractors were booked into hotels and motels in Augusta, or anywhere else there was accommodation in Augusta. But Calum was too tight to put us up in Augusta, so John and I would drive down together. The long days took their toll, leaving home at 4.30 am and arriving back home between eight and nine at night.

Construction of the Beenup mine had already started, and other contractors had dug the dredge pond and clay-tailings disposal dams already. Our job was to build pads for their buildings, along with doing a bit of rehabilitation work in the borrow pits.

John drove the digger and I drove an old D6C direct-drive swampy dozer. For an old machine, it could push. It had a hand clutch but no decelerator pedal. I would throw the clutch lever forward to disengage, then pull a second lever to select either forward or reverse, pull my hand clutch back – the nose would rear up – and away I'd go! The only downside was that it had no air-con. Being summer, inside the cab was a cross between a furnace and a dust bowl. It was okay when we were constructing the building pads because the water cart kept the dust down.

When the pads were finished, I wound up reinstating one of the borrow pits. Topsoil was carted in by a couple of 633D elevator scrapers and dumped roughly, then I would push the topsoil up the batters.

One Friday afternoon, after cooking in the dozer all day, I drove over to pick John up. As I pulled up, I could see him smashing his grease gun over the tracks of his digger.

'Hey, John,' I yelled, 'that's not the company image we're looking for, mate. You'll give us a bad name.'

'Stuff your bloody company image,' he said, as he fired his broken grease gun into the scrub. We both started laughing, but all those 16-hour days meant tempers were flaring.

The following day, I was sweltering in the dozer as usual. I wore a dust mask and was covered from head to foot in topsoil dust, which stuck to my sweat. By lunchtime, the mercury was rising and so was my temper. I was pushing topsoil along the side of a steep batter when my door swung open with a bang, cracking the bottom window of the door. I thought, piece of junk – who cares?

About an hour later the top door window rattled out and smashed on the track. Heck, how am I going to explain that one to Calum? I wondered.

By three o'clock, I'd had enough of cooking in the cab and choking in dust, mask or no mask. Out of desperation, I tried opening the right-hand window, which swung out on a hinge. The window had a handle like a Land Rover's, which you twisted down to open, but, like the rest of the dozer, it didn't work. The window handle was frozen solid.

A 633 elevator scraper dumped its load right beside me in a cloud of dust. Swearing and fighting to open the window, I grabbed my steel grease gun off the floor and took a flying swing at the door handle to smack it down.

Whack, whack, whack! Crack! I'd misfired with the grease gun and broken the window.

Oh bugger. Now I had some real explaining to do.

When John came to pick me up in the ute at the end of the day, he said, 'Phew, Mick, you're rough on the gear. Look at all those broken windows. That's not the company image we're trying to portray …' and we both cracked up laughing.

* * *

With all the time I spent driving between Bunbury and Beenup, I had my share of near-misses on the back roads. Sometimes I took a shortcut through Sues Road, which an old, mostly gravel logging road that was about to be widened and tar-sealed for the road trains to cart out of Beenup back to Bunbury. Kangaroos were a problem. They weren't so bad in the daylight, but early in the morning, they were everywhere.

You were asking for trouble. It wasn't hard to wind up with a furry hood ornament if you weren't paying attention.

Kangaroos mostly come out at night and they have no road sense whatsoever. They will hop across a paddock, flat out, and jump the fence right out in front of your vehicle before you can blink. The outcome is either a stoved-in mudguard or a nice 'V' imprint in your bonnet.

My biggest fear, though, was hitting an emu. Because of their long legs and big body, they can roll over the bonnet and through your windscreen, which is what happened to a mate of mine.

'Yeah, Mick,' he said. 'I just picked up my brand-new Holden ute. She was a beauty. Every two years I get a new one from the company and I can choose what I want. I picked it up from the car dealer and took it for a spin out past Collie. Had me window down having a quiet ciggie, just cruisin' along in a daydream. Then out the corner of my eye I spot an emu. Too late – bang! It hit the front corner of my brand new ute, and its body rolls up over the bonnet. I was in luck, though, as it hit my driver's side corner window, right on the pillar.'

'Man, you were lucky!' I cut in, picturing the scene.

'Nah, Mick. Brassed me right off. The emu's long neck and head snapped right round on impact and went straight through my open driver's window. Its head tore off and landed in me lap, knocking me ciggie out of me hand, down into my crutch – and I was wearing shorts. The bloody insides of its head splattered all over my brand-new dashboard and new roof lining, and I burnt one of my knackers by the time I pulled over to sort myself out.'

Thankfully, I never did run into an emu, but my tally for kangaroos was five for the year. Just as well for steel roo bars.

The last time I drove down to Beenup was early on a Monday morning. I'd already worked more than 112 hours for the week, including Sunday, and I was past tired. I even had the window right down so I could stick my head out in the hope the cool air would keep me awake.

The last thing I remember was turning off the old logging road onto the highway. When I came to, I looked around, confused and disorientated. It took me a minute or two to work out that I was down in a big open drain on the opposite side of the road. Luckily, no one had been coming the other way when I wandered over onto the wrong side of the road. Even luckier was the fact the ute hadn't rolled.

That was it for me. After getting the ute out of the drain, I turned around and drove home. I rang Calum when I got there and told him to stick his seven-days-a-week job. He wasn't happy, but that was his problem.

The Beenup mineral-sand mine only operated for two years instead of the 20 that had been proposed. It was shut down because of high levels of clay and sand abrasiveness causing plant maintenance issues, which forced the plant to run at only 60 per cent. The dredge, which was one of the largest in the world at the time, could work down to 40 or 50 metres deep.

By the time Beenup closed, the government had contributed $44 million to the upgrade of various road networks and bridges, including Sues Road, and by the time Beenup was reinstated, BHP's foray into mineral-sand mining had cost them $300 million.

18

Anyone got a plug on them?

CALUM WAS KEEN TO keep me, so he sent me to another site. The job was on a huge project next to the harbour in Bunbury, and involved building an 80,000-tonne reinforced-concrete oil-storage facility in a casting basin. To create the casting basin, a hole approximately three football fields wide and 15 metres deep – 12 metres of which was below sea level – had to be dug, with only a seawall separating it from the harbour.

Once the giant hole had been dug, the concrete gravity structure was built within it. The giant rectangular concrete box had a huge shaft, 11 metres in diameter, at each corner, which rose up to about 70 metres. The stacks could be seen all over Bunbury.

When the facility was complete, the seawall was to be dredged out slowly. Then water would fill the casting basin to float the 80,000-tonne concrete structure. Once it was afloat, the structure would be towed 1700 kilometres up to the Wandoo oil field on the North West Shelf and sunk to a depth of 55 metres, using 45,000 tonnes of iron ore ballast to sink the structure on to the seabed, with the four shafts just sticking out of the ocean.

A barge carrying the 6500-tonne oilrig platform from Singapore would then arrive to lower the platform down to the four big stacks of the structure. When the platform was attached, one of the stacks would be used for drilling into the seabed. Up to 400,000 barrels of oil could be stored down in the concrete gravity structure under the ocean.

John and I started on the harbour project at the same time. He was digging down in the casting basin hole and I was up top digging heaps of open drains and building up their laydown area with my 22-tonner.

Calum also hired a new bloke, Chris, to drive one of our excavators. After working a couple of months, Chris walked up to me and said, 'Mick, I'm just going down the road to buy a meat pie.'

'Yeah, rightio, Chris. No worries, mate,' I said, and thought nothing of it.

Two hours later, still no Chris.

Three hours, he still wasn't back.

In the end, he didn't come back – he snatched it.

It became a standing joke between John and me. If I was having a bad day, I would say: 'John, you know, I might as well go and buy a meat pie.'

One Friday towards Christmas, Calum was transporting one of the diggers down to Capel. It was a foggy morning and there'd been a bushfire in the area, so there was smoke and patches of fog mixed together. He was coming down a winding tree-lined country road when he hit a bad patch of smog and couldn't see ahead. He veered off the road and ploughed between two big gumtrees with low branches, which tore off the roof of his cab at steering-wheel height.

I don't know if the digger was properly chained down on the float. It slid round sideways on the deck but, fortunately, didn't come off.

Calum offloaded the digger over the side, pulled the truck out from the trees back onto the road with the digger, picked up his shattered roof and other bits of broken fibreglass, threw them on the back and drove the roofless truck back to the yard. It would have been a sight to see him cruising along behind the wheel, wearing his dark green teardrop Ray-Ban fighter pilot shades. Unbelievably, he didn't have a scratch on him.

That night, John and I pulled into Calum's yard to pick up our holiday pay and to have a few beers for the end of year break-up. Lo and behold! The gates were locked and there was no sign of Calum. We took one look at the damaged truck and thought he must have been badly injured, which is why he wasn't at home. Fair enough. It looked serious.

We rang him to see how he was. As it turned out, he was halfway down the line, heading to a camping ground to start his holidays.

I hung up the phone and turned to John: 'Yep, he's okay, but the bad news is, he's gone off on holiday.'

'But what about our holiday pay? I need it,' cried John.

'It goes to show what he thinks of us, eh, mate?' I replied. 'Come on, let's have our own Christmas party.'

We headed back to town and spent the evening at the Captain Bunbury Hotel then, much later, staggered off to a nightclub.

I woke up feeling a bit seedy the next morning. But on the bright side, it was Saturday and we were going to be breaking up for Christmas after today.

When I got to the job site, John looked like death warmed up. Pale-faced and quiet, he climbed into the cab of his digger and trundled off down into the casting basin, and I walked my digger over to the laydown area.

About 10 minutes later, John and his digger trundled back up out of the hole and headed across the road to the stockpile area. A ute pulled up beside me. It was Greg, the leading hand. We had some good bosses on the site. All of them were laid back and most of them had come over from Brisbane.

I slid my window open and leaned my head out. 'Gidday, Greg, aren't we the epitome of health this morning?' I said, giving him a big smile with my teeth clenched.

He looked at me suspiciously: 'I just sent John over to the stockpile out of harm's way. He's drunk.'

'Drunk, you say? Well, I never! That's disgusting, turning up for work under the influence. What was he thinking? That's not the company image we're trying to uphold,' I said, trying not to laugh.

Greg was still looking at me suspiciously. 'You're slurring, Mick.'

'Nah, I'm not.'

'Yes, you are,' he said as he and opened my cab door. 'Pooh, you stink like a brewery. You reek of Bundy rum.'

'Well, I might have had one or two refreshments last night – that I remember,' I admitted.

'Exactly what time did you blokes get home last night?'

'Oh, about two hours ago.'

'Right, go and join your partner in crime out of harm's way – and don't fall off the stockpile and kill yourselves while you're at it,' he said as he walked off shaking his head.

One evening not long after Christmas, John phoned me. He was drunk and had wound himself up about us not getting our holiday pay. Calum was back from holiday by then, so John had paid him a visit and banged on his door late one night and gave him an earful in no uncertain terms. He let him have it, to the point where Calum almost got dropped. That was the beginning of the end for me and John. We were now on Calum's radar.

When we started back at work, Calum had hired a young bloke called Ross. He had worked on a few big construction projects and was switched on. When he asked us what our pay rates were, I said, 'Same as what we've always been on.'

'Well, you shouldn't be,' he said, then rattled off all these allowances we were supposed to be getting.

'Wouldn't have a clue about construction rates,' I replied.

Ross went and saw the bosses on our behalf, and Greg turned up shortly afterwards.

'Did you blokes get your new boots and jackets?' he asked.

'Don't know anything about that,' I replied.

'If you don't mind me asking, Mick, what pay rates are you blokes on?'

I told him.

'Is that right?' he said, frowning. Then he told me what they were paying everyone else on the site. 'Sounds like he's pocketing the difference. I'll soon sort that out. Come with me, boys.'

We wandered over to see the site storeman and Greg told him to sort us out with boots and work gear. Then he said to us, 'This gear and your back pay will be coming straight off his next machine-hire claim, whether he likes it or not.'

I turned to Greg and said, 'So, for the summer of ninety-five, John and I will be sporting new company jackets and boots, and for fashion accessories, we'll be carrying new designer lunchboxes and Thermos combos by Stanley.'

Greg grinned. 'Pair of clowns,' he said, and walked off.

True to his word, we got back-paid. Calum wasn't happy about it.

About two weeks later, Calum found an excuse to take John's work ute off him, so John had to use his own car. Then he used some excuse to swap my work ute for his old farm hack, which was a Holden one-tonner ute complete with hay bales still on the back.

As I was driving home around the estuary to Australind in my 'new' farm hack, a car pulled out in front of me and I slammed on the brakes. The brakes grabbed on one side and I nearly shot off the road and into a power pole. I was fizzing when I got home.

Next morning, I walked out to find a pool of oil that had dripped from the ute all over the pavers in my driveway. I fumed as I climbed inside to start it, but the battery was dead.

'Right, that's enough of mickey-taking from this bloke. This ute's a death trap,' I yelled, as I climbed back out and booted the driver's door shut as hard as I could, then booted it a couple more times just to make sure it was closed properly, leaving a big 'V' in the driver's door.

I walked inside and rang Calum. 'If you haven't come to pick up this rust bucket and get it off my property by the time I get home, I'll put a match to your precious hay bales.'

Needless to say, the ute had disappeared by the time I got home.

* * *

After a day off in Perth, I caught the tail end of a news item about something that had happened on the job at the casting basin. I called John to find out the details.

He told me he'd been parked on a ramp having his smoko. As he'd glanced around the casting basin, he'd noticed Greg in what looked like an argument with one of the bosses. They were pointing at the sea wall, which was all that separated the casting basin from the harbour. At this stage, the casting basin was about seven metres below sea level, with another five metres to go,

Greg was pointing at what looked like groundwater leaking down the side of the sea bund wall. That in itself was nothing unusual: groundwater leaked out all around the casting basin, running into sumps from open drains cut into the berms. The floor was always wet, and we were starting to get into this slippery, hard black clay. It was tight to dig out. Whenever I tried to scoop out a bucketful, the bucket stayed still and the digger slid straight up to it. The clay instantly went to slop once it was dug out of the ground, so we couldn't even sit on it. With mud and slop plus groundwater running out of the banks, it would be hard to tell if there was a leak in the wall or not.

John heard Greg yelling, 'You'd better get everyone and the gear out of the hole.'

Luckily, there were only three machines in there at the time: two diggers – one of which was John's – and a small wheel loader parked at the bottom of the hole.

One of the bosses yelled back, 'Nah, just get the D10 dozer to come down and push a bit of dirt up against the leak in the wall.'

'Push a bit of dirt? Push a bit of dirt! I think you'd better get everyone out of the hole now. Look! It's getting faster,' Greg yelled.

'Quick! Get everyone out,' shouted one of the bosses.

Everyone bolted up the ramp and out of the casting basin hole. John rattled his digger flat-out up the ramp. A young labourer over the back of the job didn't have time to make it to the ramp and ran straight up the slope as the wall holding back the harbour opened up and a wall of seawater came crashing in.

The parked digger took the full brunt of the wall of water and was pushed over onto its side. The wheel loader was end-for-ended over to the other side of the floor by the force. Meanwhile, the young labourer was still scrambling frantically up the bank, looking over his shoulder at the seawater slowly rising up out of the hole to meet him. Thankfully, the young fella made it out okay, as did everyone else.

It took a few weeks to pump out the water and repair the sea wall. This time, they keyed a slot down the middle of the wall with a big clam shell on a crane then they filled the key with bentonite to seal any leaks that might leach through the wall. That's why it breached: seawater had seeped through the limestone underneath the wall.

After the wall was repaired, there were no more incidents, but it still didn't feel right knowing that a large body of water was only a few metres away, especially when we had got down to a depth of 12 metres. Everyone kept peering over to the sea wall, looking for leaks after that.

The harbour job was a challenging project. It was a great day when it was finally completed and we sat high up on a hill to watch the towering concrete gravity structure being towed out of the harbour on the start of its 1700-kilometre trip to its final resting place off the Dampier coast.

It wasn't all plain sailing, though. On the way up the coast, a towline was snapped in the rough seas and the 81,000 tonnes of structure almost pulled the tugboats backwards towards the shoreline. But they managed to fly someone by helicopter on to the concrete gravity structure and reattach the towline.

19

Living the dream

AFTER WE'D FINISHED THE harbour project, I worked briefly at Tarmoola mine site near Leonora and stayed living in Bunbury. There, I bumped into Mackie, my old dirt boss from Kurara, who I hadn't seen for about seven years. He told me he had a crook ticker, so he wasn't allowed to be a dirt boss anymore. His new job involved running around with a clipboard, testing everyone for competencies on dump trucks and machines.

He hadn't changed. In the morning, he tested me on a 100-tonne Komatsu dump truck. 'Okay, Mick, let's go for a spin,' he said. 'Loosen up, mate, loosen up. No white knuckles on the steering wheel, please.'

I pulled up to the digger and shot backwards, under the bucket, but the digger driver was too slow lifting it. There was a loud bang as the back of my tray clipped the digger bucket.

'Did he just hit you with his bucket, Mick? Did he? Did he?' yelled Mackie, all excited.

'Don't raise that blood pressure, Mackie. I don't want to have to give you mouth-to-mouth!'

'Bugger off, Bellamy. Your driving will kill me first!'

Mackie looked around the mine site with a professional eye from his dickey seat beside me in the cab. 'Look how he's set up,' he said, pointing to one of the diggers sitting up on a bench.

Our company had just taken over the contract, so everyone was new. 'Look at the state of that haul road and look at those windrows. They need building up. This dirt boss doesn't know what he's doing,' he spluttered.

At that moment, Ted, the dirt boss, called me up on the radio: 'Copy, Mick. Head over to Jonno's digger and cart out of there.'

Me and Mackie look at each other. 'Who's Jonno when he's at home?' Mackie asked.

I called up: 'Copy, Ted. Who's Jonno? Over.'

'Another digger driver. Who else do you think he is, Mick?'

'Yeah, Ted, I figured that one out, mate. But you've got four diggers running – which one is Jonno on?'

'The bloody Hitachi,' he answered.

'Okay, Ted, we're getting warmer. There's two Hitachis, mate. Which one?'

By now, Mackie was biting at the bit. 'What a bloody circus,' he said. 'That clown doesn't know what he's doing.'

The next day, Ted stuck me on the Sterling road-truck water cart. When I started the truck, the red fuel-warning light came on. No problem, I thought, I'll just call up the service truck.

'Copy, service truck,' I called.

Ted cut in on the two-way: 'Why do you want the service truck?'

'Umm, to get some fuel. My warning light's on.'

'You just keep going and stop mucking round. He'll catch up with you along the way. Over.'

Well, about three-quarters of an hour later, there was still no service truck. I was starting to sweat it a bit. I didn't want to run out of fuel. That was when I spotted the service truck over the other side of the pit, filling up the drill rigs, so I headed over there in the water cart.

'Sorry, mate,' Tom, the serviceman, said when I pulled up. 'I clean forgot all about you.'

After Tom fuelled me up, I climbed back into the cab and the radio crackled into life. 'Copy, Mick,' came Ted's voice. 'Who told you to go over there and stand around yakking? Over.'

'Well, Ted,' I replied, 'I thought I'd use my noggin, as my fuel light's been on for over an hour.'

I was starting to get brassed off with this clown and got the impression he loved the sound of his own voice. He was about five-foot nothing and middle-aged and he wore a big, shiny CAT buckle. Yee-hah!

'Copy, Mick. Do a run down into the pit. Over,' said Ted.

I pulled up under the standpipe sock and filled the water cart right to the top until it overflowed and started heading down into the pit. The three-speed automatic Sterling truck was far too small for the mine site, but it had a big tank on the back.

This was my first time watering the haul road down into the bottom of the pit. I took it quietly as I started heading down into the pit. The road had a fairly steep grade, so I put the exhaust brake on to hold the truck as I ground down into the pit.

Next minute, the truck started to take off, getting faster and faster, and I began to panic. Before long, it was fair-sailing down the haul road. I kept pushing the buttons on the dash to try to change it down a gear, but to no avail.

My mind was racing. Oh no, oh no! Do I jump out and let it crash? Nah. Can't jump out. I was fair-motoring down the haul road by then and I couldn't have jumped off if I'd wanted to.

I grabbed the two-way radio: 'Runaway truck heading into pit. Could all dump trucks pull over and stop? Repeat. Stop.'

Ted called up: 'Mick, halfway down on your left is a side road. Turn off there and you should be able to pull up and stop.'

I sailed around a couple of bends, spotted the side road and peeled off. To my relief, I managed to pull up slowly then grind to a halt.

Just as I was trying to get my breath back, Ted's voice came through the radio again: 'Yeah, I forgot to tell you, Mick, only half-fill that water cart when entering this pit. The brakes won't hold with that weight.'

* * *

From Tarmoola, I headed back to Bunbury, where I got a job with a local crowd. The boys were a bunch of larrikins always having a laugh at someone's expense. Alonso, our Italian loader driver, was permanently high. I'm still not sure he was high on life or high-as-a-kite high. though. He would drive his loader around the site at 100 miles an hour, scraping the cats' eyes off the road as he screamed past you, just missing your toes with his loader bucket, all the while singing at the top of his voice. Nature had its compensations, though – Alonso had long, black dreadlocks and was the spitting image of Johnny Depp. He was a magnet for women.

It was summertime. We were laying a sewer main down in Busselton, about 50 kilometres south of Bunbury. In those days, we could just throw the sand out on the road for Alonso to backfill the trench with later.

Working with us was Mark, a young pipe-setter. He was a super well-mannered, quietly spoken guy with blond hair and was a charmer with the ladies. Also on that job was Tim, our subbie Bobcat driver. He was a stocky bloke and just as bad as the other two. His Bobcat was always parked up someone's driveway at lunchtime. Rounding out the crew was Calvino, our long-suffering Italian foreman who had to put up with this crazy mob.

We were right in suburbia, digging the verge and crossing people's driveways. As we got up to each driveway, we would dig straight through it, if it was gravel, or plunk under the driveway if it was paved or concreted. Plunking was a method of working the pipes through the sand under the driveway using a six-inch pipe and a slightly longer four-inch pipe with a hole cut in for a handle. The crew would lay the six-inch pipe flat down in the bottom of the sewer trench, up against the end of the trench we were about to tunnel under, place the four-inch pipe inside the six-inch pipe, and someone would get on their hands and knees and straddle the six-inch pipe to steady it. Next, they would grab the slot in the four-inch pipe and thrust and twist, thrust and twist the four-inch pipe into the sandy ground.

Slowly sand would work its way out from the end of the four-inch pipe, which would now be tunnelling under the driveway. When the four-inch pipe was nearly flush with the six-inch pipe, you would stop and twist the six-inch pipe into the hole that you had just tunnelled and carry on the sequence until you'd plunked through to the other side of the driveway.

By that stage, you'd be soaked with sweat, have dry, powdery sand stuck all over your clothes and down the back of your neck. And if you were unlucky, like we were, the trench would be infested with sugar-ant nests in the sand banks – and along with the swarms of March flies, they were biting and stinging the living daylights out of us.

We all took a turn at plunking. We would use an old steel pipe if we couldn't plunk beneath a driveway. One day me and Mark were working together. I had just pushed the steel casing under a driveway with the excavator, then started digging down the other side to find the end of the steel casing.

I dug along the top off the steel pipe and exposed the end.

Mark climbed down into the trench and stood on top of the casing, spotting me.

'Hey, Mick, can you dig down the front of the pipe so I don't have to shovel it?' he asked.

'Yeah, no worries, you lazy sod. Just spot me in,' I replied.

My drainage bucket was long and narrow, and Mark stood directly behind it. All I could see was my cutting edge and Mark's head and arms sticking out above the bucket.

Mark spotted me in with a wave of his hand.

Slowly, slowly I crept the cutting edge of my bucket closer and closer to the bottom of the steel pipe.

Next minute, his hand shot skywards and made odd, erratic movements, then he began to make unusual moaning sounds and his face became red and contorted.

As I pulled my bucket away, he stopped and gave me a strange look.

'Did I miss a bit, Mark?' I asked then curled my bucket back to have another go.

Immediately, there was more arm waving and moaning. This time, I worked out what was wrong and swung my bucket out of the way.

'Mark, tell me that you didn't have your work boots hanging over the front of that steel pipe. You wouldn't be that dumb, would you?' I said.

'Yes, Mick,' he whispered through clenched teeth.

The back of my bucket had caught the tops of his steel-capped boots and rolled them over the lip of the steel pipe. Lucky for him, it hadn't sliced his toes off.

'Oh, shit! Get those boots off before your feet swell up,' I said. I jumped out of the cab to help him unlace his work boots, fully expecting all of his toes to be broken.

Mark pulled his socks off. His toes were green and black.

Calvino had heard the ruckus and came over to find out what was going on. 'What-a happen, Mick?'

'Poor Mark guided my digging bucket onto his toes,' I explained.

'Well, that's-a bit-a silly now, wasn't it, Mark? You won't-a be-a chasing the beautiful ladies for a while,' Calvino said, with a lopsided grin.

Mark refused Calvino's offer to take him to the doctor, so, instead, spent the next week hobbling around.

Each morning, we made him take his socks off so we could inspect the changing colours of his toes: from black to green to yellow. I still thought he should have seen a doctor, and I felt bad about it.

A short while later, a couple of subbies came onto the job to do some dewatering. They had already sunk their spears in the ground and laid out the manifold pipe beside my digger on the blindside.

The subbies were up the other end, bent over, tweaking their taps, which were all along the manifold pipe, and slowly working their way towards me. I didn't think much of it.

At lunchtime, we all sat in the shade under some peppermint trees on someone's front lawn. The subbies were as quiet as mice and one of them was gently rubbing his forehead and staring at me.

'Got a headache, mate?' I asked. 'You fellas are pretty quiet.'

Alonso cracked up laughing: 'That's a good one, Mick!'

'What's so funny, Alonso?' I asked.

'You know what happened,' one of the subbies said.

'What are you on about, mate?' I had no idea what he was on about.

By this time, Alonso was just about wetting himself. 'Didn't you see it, Mick? It was a classic. These two clowns went to turn the manifold taps on right beside your digger's blindside and you slewed around and bowled both of them right over with your counterweight. Man, it was funny,' he said.

'What? I got you fellas in the noggin with my counterweight?' I asked, surprised – then cracked up laughing. I had no sympathy. If they were dumb enough to walk on my blindside while I was digging with the sun in my eyes, then they were pretty much asking for it.

That afternoon, I began craning a manhole riser in with Mark and Calvino, when I noticed a little boy walking up to Alonso's loader.

Alonso climbed down the ladder.

'Hello,' the little fellow said to Alonso. 'My mum thought you might like some grapes,' he said, as he handed a big plastic bag to Alonso.

Meanwhile, his mum was standing outside number 24 giving a big, cheery wave and a smile.

Alonso looked at the little boy. 'Nah, don't like grapes. Tell your mum to bake me some blueberry muffins. I like blueberry muffins.'

The little boy turned to his mum, who was a fair way down the street, and yelled at the top of his voice: 'Mum, Mum, he doesn't like grapes. He wants blueberry muffins.'

'Oh, okay,' she called then gave another cheery wave and walked back inside her house.

Next day all the boys vanished at lunchtime, leaving just me and Calvino sitting in the shade. He pulled a piece of straw out the corner of his mouth that he was using to pick his teeth, looked at his watch, and said, 'It's a-bloody quarter-to-one and still they are-a not-a back.'

One o'clock came around. Still the boys weren't back.

By quarter-past-one, Calvino was fuming: 'Mick, this-a outfit is a bloody madhouse. Mark's a-limping around, chasing bikinis down at Busselton Wharf, while bloody Tim's a-Bobcat is-a parked in the carport of number two. Alonso's loader is-a parked up-a the bloody driveway of number 24 supposedly eating-a blueberry muffins. I don't-a think so! How's a bloke-a supposed to-a lay pipe when most-a of my crew is a-bonking half of-a Busselton?' he said despairingly, waving his hands in the air.

After work we would all pile into our little dual cab truck and head to the nearest drive-in bottleshop.

'How can I help you blokes?' asked the young bottleshop attendant one day. He'd come out and was standing outside the window of our truck.

'Please could I have four stubbies of Emu bitter,' asked Mark.

'I'll have-a six-pack of-a Swan lager,' said Calvino.

'Yeah, a couple of Crownies, mate,' I asked.

Then Alonso poked his dreadlocked head out the window. 'Heh, mate, give me five dollars' worth of beer, thanks,' he said. 'That's all I've got on me.'

'Five dollars of what, mate?' asked the attendant.

'I don't know – what's cheap and on special?' asked Alonso.

The attendant gave Alonso a long, pained look. 'Well, VB's on special this week,' he said.

'Nah, I don't like VB. Gives me gas,' said Alonso. 'What else is on special, bud?

'What about Carlton Bitter?' said the attendant, with an icy stare.

'Carlton Bitter? Don't mention Carlton Bitter, mate. Last time I drank that stuff, I was hopping on the throne for days and left with a burning ring of fire.'

'What do you bloody want, you drongo?' exploded the bottleshop attendant.

'Just taking a lend of you. Give us a six pack of Jimmy Beams and a bag of chippies, thanks, mate,' said Alonso.

And off we went with our roadies for the trip back to Bunbury.

* * *

After we had finished the sewer job in Busselton, me and Alonso started clearing some bush for a new catchment at the fertiliser works pond beside the Preston River out the back of Picton.

I started pushing over the trees while Alonso was clearing the bush and stacking up the logs. I was driving an old Kato 20-tonne digger. It had no air-con, so, given it was a stinking hot summer's day, I had the door and windows open and the sun roof was up.

It was getting near lunchtime as I dug round the roots of a gnarly, old red gum. I extended my dipper arm up as high as it could reach, dug my rock teeth into the trunk of the gumtree and sent it on its way in a shower of leaves and swirling dust.

As I waited for the dust to clear, a bee stung me on the back of the neck, then another one stung me on the top of my head.

'Ouch, ouch, ouch,' I cried out as I was stung again.

A gust of wind blew the dust away, and in front of me I saw a huge swarm of angry bees flying out of the old red gum and heading my way.

'Oh, no! I yelled as I bailed out of the cab, sprinted past Alonso, jumped a log, side-stepped a grass tree and bolted off into the bush, waving my hands frantically and swatting bees away as I went. All the while, Alonso was beside himself with laughter at my predicament, as he sat watching on in his nice, air-conditioned Samsung loader.

The bees had stopped chasing me by the time Alonso pulled up on his loader. I was bent over double, huffing and puffing after my marathon bush bash.

'That was a bloody classic, Mick,' he said, wiping away his tears of laughter. 'Wait till I tell the boys!'

'Yeah, ha, ha, Alonso. Could you do me a favour and fish around in my hair and pull out a few bee stings, mate?'

'Ewww! You want me to feel around in that greasy mop of yours?'

'Yeah, if you could, mate,' I replied.

'Yeah, alright,' he said. 'But make sure no one's watching. I don't want anyone to get the wrong idea about you and me, mate, if you know what I mean ... Mmm, what soft, shiny hair you have!'

'Clear off, Alonso. Stand around the front of me where I can see you, mate, so you don't get any funny ideas.'

'Don't know what all the fuss is about, Mick. A few little, tiny bee stings. What a blouse!'

We crept back to the Kato digger, which still had the boom and dipper arm high up in the air and the motor screaming away at full revs. We cautiously peered round an old jarrah tree.

'Now, where are those pesky little sods?' I wondered out loud.

'They're still brassed off with you, Mick, you home wrecker,' Alonso said. 'The bees are still swarming. Look over there,' he added, pointing in the direction of the swarm.

'Ah, blow it. Let's put the nose bag on and leave the bees to quieten down a bit,' I said, and we crept off, leaving the old Kato screaming its ring out.

After lunch, Alonso hopped in his loader and pushed the old red gum away from the digger, then I climbed into the cab and pushed the throttle lever back to idle position. Finally – silence.

Later that afternoon, I was covered in thick dust with sweat rolling off me. Alonso had his window open, having a smoke – and probably not a legal one, I thought, going by the rude song he was singing to himself.

He scooped up an old jarrah I had just bowled and carted it over to the log heap, where he stacked it.

Suddenly his rude song stopped and was replaced by, 'Ow, aagh, you little pest. Aagh, you little sod!'

His door flew open and he bailed out of the loader and sprinted past me, his dreadlocks flowing behind him. On his face was that determined look an athlete has when he's going for gold.

Now I was the one cracking up laughing as I watched Alonso flapping his arms and swatting at his dreadlocks before he disappeared into the bush.

A short while later, he gingerly walked out of the bush. 'Hey, Mick,' he said sheepishly, 'can you pull a bee sting out of my hair, mate?'

'What a fluff, Alonso. One tiny bee sting. I got stung four times. Ugh! Do I really have to touch these greasy dreadlocks?' I asked, while holding one up with the tips of my fingers and peering through his hair. 'Mmm Alonso, you Italian stallion. What product do you use? Smells like something deadly, mmm ...'

'Mick, if you touch me anywhere but my head, I will break your fingers,' he replied, and we both cracked up laughing.

20
Bunbury born and raised

ROCCO SPINETTI HAD JUST finished laying a couple of stormwater lines. At first glance, Rocco looked as Italian as could be – slight of build with curly black hair and an olive complexion – but when he spoke, it was with a deep Aussie twang.

He was a funny bloke with a dry sense of humour. He could crack a joke and keep a straight face, with his permanent scowl, dark, piercing eyes and bushy monobrow making his jokes even funnier.

'Hey, Mick, our crowd has just scored a job in town, down the northern end of Victoria Street,' he said one day, all excited, 'right outside the Captain Bunbury.'

The job was to widen Victoria Street, build new roundabouts and parking bays, tidy up Guppy Park and add some new pavers and tree planter pits to the streetscape from the corner of Victoria Street and Clifton Streets, up past the Captain Bunbury Hotel and the old Port Pottery building to the base of

Marlston Hill. This was a distance of about 250 metres. The tank farms around Marlston Hill had slowly disappeared and would soon give way to the new housing developments that would spring up all around the hill in years to come.

While I was working with him, we often heard the toot of a car horn and someone calling out, 'Hey, Rocco,' as they drove past. Every time it happened, he would wave by sticking his arm in the air, bent at the elbow but with one finger pointing at the sky, like an AFL referee. Then he would give a little twitch of his finger out to the side. If anyone walked past and said 'Gidday', they'd get the same one-fingered wave while his monobrow gave a little twitch of recognition.

I was curious to know how this bloke knew so many people. 'Gee, you're popular, Rocco. Just about everyone in Bunbury knows you,' I remarked one day after someone in a car had called out to him.

'Born and raised in Bunbury, Mick. Either went to school with them or worked with them.' Bunbury was a close-knit town.

The end of town where we were working was quite barren and run down. There was a rundown guest house called Yanget House, across from the Captain Bunbury Hotel, where a few blokes who were down on their luck would sit out front and watch us.

One of them was a stooped-over old bloke with a bushy beard and a mop of grey, spiky hair. He looked a bit like a werewolf, so the boys nicknamed him Londy after the Warren Zevon song 'Werewolves of London'. Even though Londy walked with a limp, he used to wander all over Bunbury and he was well looked after by the local shopkeepers.

One day, we saw Londy limping down the street. He had his arm in a cast.

'Hey Mick, did you hear about Londy?' Alonso said. 'He was behind Trafs Bar fossicking in a big industrial skip bin. You know, the ones with the heavy steel lids. He was on his tiptoes with his arm over the side of the skip having a scavenge, when he knocked the latch holding up the steel lid, which dropped on his arm, pinning him there till a bouncer found him later on, hanging out of the skip.'

The local shopkeepers rallied to look after Londy over the following few days. He suddenly had a new flowery shirt and new shoes, and he sported a new haircut and trimmed beard.

After work one day, we all piled into the Captain Bunbury pub for a few coldies, It wasn't long before I got the munchies and wandered off down the road to buy a couple of kebabs.

As I walked out of the kebab shop, I bumped into Londy standing outside. 'Do you want a feed, mate?' I said as I offered him one of my kebabs.

'Nah, don't like kebabs and I'm not hungry. Got any money for beer?'

Taken aback, I replied, 'Nah, mate. If I give you any money, you'll probably wind up breaking the other arm.'

He grunted and gave me a lop-sided smile.

Victoria Street was really taking shape. Most of the pavers were down and I'd just finished digging out the ring beams for the new roundabouts. One of our subbies, Jacko, had shown up with his Bobcat to level off some topsoil to finish Guppy Park, ready for the new turf that was arriving the following day.

Jacko had brought his metal detector with him. 'You never know, Mick,' he said, 'Guppy Park is an old part of Bunbury with a lot of history. Once I cut off the old turf, you never know what I might find buried underneath it.'

Guppy Park had a penny arcade years ago, so for a little park it held a lot of secrets.

Along with a bunch of old coins, Jacko found a set of dog tags from the First World War. He contacted a local historian, who traced the family of the soldier the tags had belonged to. It turned out that soldiers had camped at Guppy Park before they embarked on troopships to head for the war. In a bit of good news, the soldier who had lost his tags had survived the war and come home to his family. The story of the missing dog tags even made the local newspaper.

Jacko wasn't the only one to grace the paper's pages. One night, I was sitting at home having a read of the paper and there was a picture of Rocco holding up a street sign, doing a grip and grin. You could tell he was grinning: his dark, piercing eyes had disappeared under his scowl as he stared into the camera lens. But the real giveaway was his monobrow: it had formed into the letter W. He was smiling on the inside.

The next time I saw him, I said, 'Mate, you scared the daylights out of me!'

'What are you on about, Mick?'

'The mugshot of you in the local rag,' I replied. 'I was helping you that day putting up the street sign. I never saw any photographer.'

'Well, Mick, if you stopped thinking of your stomach and skiving off ten minutes early every lunchtime, your mug might have wound up in there as well,' he said, giving his monobrow a little flutter.

A couple of months later, the same thing happened again just after he and I had finished painting a wall outside the Missions to Seamen building on the corner of Carey and Victoria streets. I was relaxing at home with my feet up on the coffee table, flicking through the local newspaper, only so see: 'Sprucing up Victoria Street with some final touches is Bunbury local, Rocco Spinetti.'

This time, he had a paintbrush in his hand and he was doing a grip and grin.

'Hey, Rocco, you tin arse, how did you manage to pull that one off? I was there all day and at lunchtime, so how did your mug end up in the local rag again?' I asked.

'Well, if you hadn't snuck off into the Captain Bunbury ten minutes early at knock-off time ... Anyway, can't help it if I've got stunningly good looks and am photogenic, mate. You're just jealous!' Rocco said, frowning while his monobrow went into spasms. Then he decided to confess: 'The reporter is a mate of mine. We went to the school together. He just rings me if he's a bit short on stories for the week, and I fill in the gaps.'

Friday was skimpies night at the Captain Bunbury Hotel, so all the boys piled in for a beer.

Propping up the bar, Jacko ordered another midi of super. As the barmaid poured the beer, he said, 'Love, do you toss?'

'Sure do, mate,' came her reply.

'Oh, you beauty,' Jacko replied, as he dug in his pants pocket for a $2 coin to toss.

'Oh, right, here we go,' he said, as he was about to toss the coin.

'Nah, mate, it's five bucks,' said the barmaid.

'Five dollars!' exclaimed Jacko. 'That's daylight robbery.'

She grinned. 'Well, my titties are worth it.'

'I don't believe it. Five dollars? Five dollars? This is outrageous!' said Jacko. 'I might have to go to the titty tribunal over this.' He turned to me. 'Hey, Mick, got any change on you, mate?'

'I got a dollar,' I replied.

'I got fifty cents,' added Rocco.

Calvino piped up: 'I got-a fifty cents as well.'

'Crikey, you two are big spenders, aren't you?' said Jacko.

Alonso and Mark made up the difference.

'Okay, love, heads or tails?' said the barmaid.

'Heads,' Jacko said – and won the toss. 'Yahoo, I win after all that,' he said. 'Okay, love, show us what you've got!'

The barmaid hoisted her tee shirt up.

'Wow, definitely worth five bucks all right. Money well spent,' said Jacko as the rest of us nodded in agreement.

A few midis later, I looked over to see Rocco telling a joke. It must have been a really funny one because his monobrow was spasming uncontrollably.

'So, Rocco, you'd have to watch it round bushfire season,' I yelled over the noise of the crowd.

'What are you dribbling on about, Mick?'

'Well, that forest of hair on your arms and legs, and that possum skin on your chest – you'd go up in a flash!'

He laughed. 'Nothing wrong with this gladiator physique. At least I'm not built like a broomstick!'

Totally unfazed, I yelled back, 'So, tell me, Rocco, at the start of each summer, do you shave a firebreak round your wrists and ankles as a precaution, mate?'

'Get lost, Mick – and it's your shout,' he replied.

At closing time, Rocco and I wandered around the back of the pub to his car.

'Hang on, Mick, just going for a slash,' he said as disappeared off into the darkness.

Sitting in his car quietly, waiting for Rocco to return, I heard voices in the dark. A show had just finished at the

Entertainment Centre and the car park was starting to get busy. I thought to myself, Should I, or shouldn't I? Yeah, why not? I leaned over and flicked the car lights on high beam. Lit up against the brick wall like it was broad daylight, was Rocco relieving himself.

'Mick, you low life, turn those bloody lights off,' he yelled, to the sound of people cheering and clapping.

I flicked the lights off, sniggering away, but unfortunately Rocco's car lights were replaced by blue flashing ones.

'What's going on here? Can't you hold your bladder until you get home, mate?' said a cop as he lit Rocco up with his spotlight. All I could see was Rocco squinting into the piercing light and trying to pull up his fly.

'Yeah, sorry, officer. Got a bit of a bladder problem,' Rocco replied.

'Bladder problem! You'll have a problem next time if I catch you – you'll be locked up. Now, move on,' the cop said to Rocco before turning towards me. 'And what sort of mate does that to his cobber?'

'Oh, sorry, Rocco. I was just leaning over to turn the key on so I could listen to the radio,' was my lame excuse.

Rocco was fuming, but he eventually got me back one weekend when we took the Australind train up to Perth. We sat at the back of a carriage with a wall behind us. I sat by the window and he had the aisle seat, and the train was full, with no spare seats.

We were just heading out of Waroona when he turned to me and said, 'I might see what sandwiches they've got.'

As he wandered off up the aisle to look for the buffet car, I noticed that the thick foam squab on Rocco's seat had pulled out slightly, so I pushed it back in. I figured the squabs had to be able to be pulled out for cleaning, so I pulled his squab right off, leaving only the base of the seat with the springs sticking out. Then I leaned over and had a peep up and down the aisle to make sure the coast was clear before stashing the squab from his seat down between the back of our seats and the wall.

Ten minutes later, he showed up with a coffee in one hand and a sandwich in the other. I was reading the paper. He took one look at his seat and said, 'All right, Mick, where's me bloody seat gone to?'

I had a quick look over the top of my newspaper: 'What are you on about, mate? It's bolted to the floor beside me.'

'Yeah, yeah, funny, but what about the other half, mate? Where'd you put it?'

'Put what? I don't know what you're on about. Nothing wrong with it. That's a perfectly good seat, so don't be so fussy, mate,' I replied, trying hard not to crack up as I hid behind my newspaper. 'Sit down, Rocco. Stop making a scene. People are starting to look. You're making the place look untidy.'

All Rocco could see was my newspaper shuddering as I tried desperately not to laugh.

'Right, Mick,' he said, 'I'm going to count to three and if my seat's not back I'm going to press the buzzer for the attendant and he'll probably boot you off the train for damaging government property.'

'It's behind the seat, mate,' I said from behind my newspaper.

Next day, travelling back to Bunbury on the train, hung over and both of us not really saying much, the lady on the intercom broke into our thoughts as she announced we would be arriving in Bunbury in five minutes' time.

As soon as the train rolled to a stop in Bunbury, Rocco grabbed his bottle of water. Then, just as the carriage doors slid open, he squeezed its contents into my lap before grabbing his bag and bolting out of the carriage and onto the platform.

As a result of his attack, my pale green shorts had turned dark green in the crotch area. Looking around frantically, I quickly stood up and pulled my suitcase down from the rack above me before crab-walking out onto the platform with my suitcase pressed up against me.

'Hey, Mick, that suitcase looks real heavy. Here, let me give you a hand. That's what friends are for,' said Rocco, as he tried wresting the case off me.

'Nah, mate, it's okay, I've got it.'

'Nah, nah, I insist,' he said, as we started a tug of war with my suitcase on the platform.

Some passengers started laughing, but I don't know if their laughter was directed at me and my wet shorts or at Rocco's spasming monobrow.

* * *

Back on the work site, the company introduced this funny bit of safety clothing called a fluoro vest.

'What's this for?' asked Rocco, as he was handed one.

'You put it on like this,' one of the foremen explained. 'It's compulsory. You must wear it.'

'Bullshit. I'm not going to wear one. I'll get hooked up with it down in the trench,' Rocco said.

'You gotta wear it, mate. Here, let me show you,' the foreman said, as he tried to put the vest on Rocco.

'Clear off, mate. Don't patronise me.'

'Sorry, Rocco, you have to wear one,' insisted the foreman.

'No, I don't,' said Rocco, and he walked off the job, never to return.

A week later we finally finished Victoria Street, and it certainly looked an improvement.

Mark jumped the fence to another company. Alonso got the boot for waving to one of his mates while driving his loader round a big roundabout on the ring road heading out of Bunbury, which isn't a crime in itself. He wasn't sacked for speeding either, even though he had the loader bouncing along in top gear.

He probably should have stayed seat-belted inside his cab to avoid getting caught, high as a kite, singing out loud and waving to his mates while standing outside the cab, hanging on to the steering wheel for dear life while his other foot was still in the cab on the accelerator. Now, that's a bit naughty.

21

Initials on a tree

IT WAS TIME FOR a change of scenery, so I started a job with Macmahon. They had won a contract down at Ludlow, building a new piece of highway linking up Sues Road, which was being widened at the time by Henry Walker Eltin as part of the Beenup mine site project for their road trains to cart back to Bunbury.

I was driving a 30-tonne Komatsu digger, stripping topsoil and digging out swampland, and I'd managed to get my older brother, Gaz, a start. He had been driving trucks down in the South West and felt like a change.

Our crowd had just bought a near-new Komatsu 22-tonner, which was a minter – not a scratch on it. The dump trucks on the site were old CAT DJB 30- and 40-tonners with cabs similar to the left-hand drive cabs on motor scrapers.

Brother Gaz was sent up the far end of the job to build silt ponds.

As he was dropping me off one morning, I cautioned him: 'Hey, Gaz, just warning ya, mate, if you're loading dump trucks, watch out when they're reversing, mate. Those trucks are noisy and sometimes they can't always hear your horn. So, keep your dipper arm straight out, ready to slam down into the tray behind the headboard – just in case – unless you want to get squashed in the seat by the dump truck.'

'Yeah, yeah, whatever. Do ya think I've got the letter D stamped on my forehead, you twat?' he replied.

A typical big-brother response, I thought.

I was lucky to be working at the Ludlow end by the Bussell Highway. After he dropped me off, brother Gaz had to weave and snake his way through five or six kilometres of dry, hungry sand, right up to the other end of the project near the Vasse Highway.

It was good to be out in the country again. We were literally going straight through farmland, which was quite green for a change. Masses of arum lilies were growing in the swampy areas, and scattered along our road formation were rows of gumtrees used for windbreaks. Most of the area around the back of Busselton was as flat as a pancake and all sand.

Our earthworks supervisor, Cam, was really laid back and nothing fazed him. He took me for a drive one day.

As he drove past a row of trees, he said, 'See these trees, Mick? Bowl them.'

We wove and slid down the partly cleared, sandy road formation. All the hard bits had been left till last.

Cam pulled the Land Cruiser up once more and nodded towards a row of stumps. 'Dig those stumps while you're at it, Mick. Then pull out that old fence line and gateway. I've spoken to the farmer about it and he's all good.'

Eventually, we pulled up alongside a big patch of arum lilies. 'See that nasty, shitty swamp down there in that little hollow?' he said. 'You're going to hack it out for me. And don't get bloody bogged. The dozer's up the other end of the job. Any problems, just give me a hoy.'

That was how Cam ran the job – he gave me about three weeks' work and left me to it. Every now and then, he'd drive past me in his Land Cruiser and give me a quick thumbs up. I would wave back and he would carry on down the formation in a cloud of dust.

At knock-off time, Gaz would follow on down the formation until he found me parked up in the digger somewhere on the side of the road.

Our five-litre drink bottles were filled with ice, and, having a wide opening, you could stuff a few beer cans inside for roadies to drink on the way home. But the only problem with that was, by the end of the week, the footwell on the passenger side of the car would be chockas with squashed beer cans. After baking in the sun for a week, the work ute stunk like a brewery.

One Monday morning, Gaz and I were running late for our Tailgate meeting which everyone had to attend. As I sped my way down the sandy formation, I looked up ahead. They had already started the Tailgate meeting. Everyone was gathered round in a semi-circle. Just for a laugh, I drove the ute straight into the middle of the group of blokes, then wound my window down and said, 'Good morning, gentlemen, are we keeping the dream alive?'

Gaz opened up the passenger door to step out, but didn't lift his foot high enough, and dragged all our empties out of the footwell. They landed with a clatter on the ground.

Cam was standing there holding his clipboard, shaking his head. 'Bloody Bellamy brothers – I don't know,' he sighed. 'Right, let's get this meeting underway. Are there any issues you boys want to bring up other than drink-driving in a company vehicle?'

Also working on the job was Harry, a nice bloke, but super straight. He had a 22-tonne Kato excavator, which was mint – a real credit to him. Harry took things very seriously. For example, we were loading out dump trucks together in a borrow pit one day. He was working near an elevated motor scraper, which was moving a topsoil stockpile. Unfortunately, the motor scraper slid off the stockpile sideways and rolled over and onto its side.

Harry called up: 'Copy Macmahons. Copy Macmahons. Is it all right to stop production? A motor scraper has just rolled over. Over.'

I replied, 'Just run over and see if the poor bloke is okay, man. Stuff the production!' He was closer.

The scraper driver was okay, but he probably had to look for another job.

On our way home one night, the smell in the ute got too much. 'Mick, pull up here,' Gaz said. I pulled up next to Harry's digger along the side of the formation.

A couple of minutes later, Gaz came out from behind Harry's shiny digger, zipping up his fly and grinning. 'His track motor is going to smell tomorrow morning,' he said, before adding: 'Hey, shall we wind up Harry for a laugh? It's about time we did some housekeeping anyway – throw us out some empty beer cans, Mike.'

Everyone on site would have to drive past Harry's digger to get out onto the Bussell Highway, so we would have to be quick. I turfed the cans out onto the ground, trying not to spill the lukewarm contents. Gaz scattered the beer cans all around the cab of Harry's digger, placed a row of them along his digger tracks, then threw the rest of them on the ground beside the formation.

I was quite impressed by the number of cans we had accumulated between us.

'Hurry up, man! What are you mucking around with now, Gaz?' I asked. 'We're going to get sprung in a minute. I can see a cloud of dust from a ute approaching.'

By then, Gaz was standing beside a new survey peg that was neatly flagged off with pink tape at the base of a row of trees which had just been trimmed back for the road formation.

'Hey, Mick,' he yelled, 'What's the name of those early explorers who disappeared in the outback?'

'What? Burke and Wills, you mean?'

'Yeah, that's them.'

I couldn't see what Gaz was up to with the survey pegs as he had his back to me and was bent over a cut-off limb, peering at something on the tree.

'Right, let's get moving,' he said, as he dove into the ute, slamming the door, while tucking a black marker pen into his top pocket.

We screamed off in a cloud of dust.

'Tell me you didn't lower the levels on that survey peg, Gaz?' I said.

'Don't be stupid. I'm not that sadistic,' he replied, trying to open a tinnie without spraying it all over the over the dash as we bounced on down the track.

On Monday morning, everyone was waiting to get the Tailgate meeting over and done with.

'Right, let's kick off,' said Cam. 'Harry, the amount of beer cans littering the site around your work area has been brought to my attention. Now, I don't mind the odd coldie being consumed on site, but please be a little more inconspicuous, okay, mate? Don't leave your bloody empties for all the world to see.'

'But, but, I don't drink,' stammered Harry.

'Yeah, yeah, I've heard all the excuses before, mate,' said Cam, winking at us.

'Right,' continued Cam, 'Ken, our surveyor, has brought to my attention that he may have found something of historical significance.'

Suddenly everyone's ears pricked up.

'Ken may have located a heritage site. He was setting up his theodolite down by where Harry's working when he noticed something on the trunk of what looked like an ancient tuart tree. On closer inspection, Ken spotted some writing blazed on the trunk.'

Everyone started to murmur.

'Well, not exactly blazed,' Cam continued. 'It read: "Burke and Bellamy were here" – but written in black marker pen.'

Cam turned to us, rolling his eyes and shaking his head as everyone laughed.

* * *

Cam pulled up in his ute, looking concerned. 'Hey, Mick, your brother's just had an accident. A dump truck's backed into the side of his cab,' he said.

'What a dickhead,' I replied. 'I warned him about dump truck drivers.'

Cam was trying not to laugh. 'The cab's a write-off, but he's okay.'

I tried to picture Gaz driving a digger with a squashed cab. It must have looked funny. I sniggered about it all day.

At knock-off time, brother Gaz pulled up in the ute, looking a bit sheepish.

'You're looking a bit sunburned, Gaz. Did you leave the door open on the digger all day, mate? Or hasn't it got a door anymore?' I started sniggering again.

'Lay off, Mike. Your day will come,' he said. Little did I know how soon that would be.

Apparently, Gaz had been pulling batters with a lot of machinery working around him, so there was a lot of noise. While he was concentrating on looking down the slope, a young bloke in a dump truck decided to back up ready for a load without waiting for the signal to back up.

Brother Gaz felt the machine shudder then something touched his left shoulder. He spun sideways in time to see the young bloke's dump tray coming through his cab. Luckily, he had the front window pinned up above him, so he was able to dive out the front of the cab.

The following morning, I made a start digging out the old swamp and loading it onto the old CAT DJB dumpers. The swamp was quite deep. I worked my way into it, digging down to find the hard ground. My dump trucks were backing down behind me. The ground stunk of stagnant water.

What had happened to Gaz was playing on my mind, so I stopped what I was doing, got out and rounded up my four dump truck drivers.

'Okay, guys, just to be on the safe side, I'll spot you fellas in by hand signal,' I told them.

'That's a bit overboard, isn't it, mate?' a young bloke piped up.

'Well, mate, shortly, you will be backing down a steep ramp and stopping on the edge of the hole – and I'll be down in that hole directly behind you, reaching up to load you. If you don't hear my horn, you might drive straight over the top of me,' I explained.

Mr Attitude piped back up again: 'Whatever, mate.'

'Look, guys, any time you're in doubt on this job and you can't see me or hear my horn, just stop. Get out to have a look if you have to. I won't bite. Probably thank you for it. We don't want another occurrence like yesterday's,' I said.

The other three blokes were all experienced drivers, so they were good about it and agreed with what I said. I wasn't too concerned about them anyway, it was just the young bloke I doubted. True to form, Mr Attitude wandered back to his dump truck, shaking his head.

We fired back up again. First down the ramp was one of the experienced blokes. I stood on my track and waved him down. Just as he got to the edge of the bank, I gave him the 'Stop' signal, then hopped back into the cab and gave him a load.

Mr Attitude was parked up, watching. He was going last.

The third truck backed down. I stared up at his rear diffs as he ground to a halt above me. I threw a load on him and off he went.

Then it was Mr Attitude's turn. He swung in, straightened up and looked in his mirror at me.

'Good, he's listened to what I've said,' I muttered under my breath.

I started spotting him back slowly. Good, good. He was taking his time. Slowly the rear end of his dump truck backed down the ramp. Steady, steady. Good. He was backing offset so he could see me still in his mirrors. Good boy. 'A bit more, a bit more,' I signalled. Cool. I gave him the 'Stop' signal.

I looked into his mirror to make sure. Yep, we'd got eye contact. I hopped back into the digger and swung right to grab a bucket full of slop. Out of the corner of my eye, to my horror, I could see Mr Attitude's dump truck heading straight over the edge at me.

As I looked up, my mind raced flat-out. I hadn't got time to put my bucket in the back of his tray to stop him. My front window was closed. I was trapped, so I couldn't bail out the front. I couldn't jump out the door – there was a dump truck bearing down on it. I couldn't slew the cab out of the way because of the long overhang of the counterweight that stuck out too far. Only one option left: I slewed full swing with my bucket into the side of his dump truck.

That stopped him for a few valuable seconds, which was just enough time to get my bucket into the back of his tray. I was dumbfounded: he had started reversing back again. I quickly slammed my bucket up against his headboard to stop him completely.

By then, I was staring at his dump tray a hand's width from my window. There have been a few times in my life when I've had near misses on machines and this was one of them.

I went from sheer terror to absolutely fizzing as I thumped my rock bucket as hard as I could behind his headboard. Then again. Thump. Thump. 'Take that, you little' – thump, thump – 'twat!' Thump. Thump.

'Wait till I throttle you, you little squirt,' I yelled as I pushed his dump truck unceremoniously forward away from my cab and jumped out.

By the time I opened his door, Mr Attitude seemed to have lost his attitude and was looking a bit pale.

I held my hand in front of his face. 'What does this mean?' I asked.

'Stop,' he stuttered.

'Well, why didn't you?' I yelled.

'I thought you wanted me to carry on,' he whispered.

'What? You thought I wanted you to run me over? Now, why would I do that, you dickhead?'

'Having a bad day, Mick?' came Cam's voice behind me. 'Saw you pounding the crap out of his headboard.'

'Nah, Cam, but this clown just tried to kill me,' I said, suddenly feeling quite shaken.

'Did he? Do you want me to send him down the road?' Cam asked.

'Yep! That might sharpen his attitude,' I replied.

Cam didn't have to think twice. 'Jump in, pal,' he said, gesturing to him to hop in the Land Cruiser.

That's what I liked about the construction industry back then. It weeded out the idiots.

22

Country life

TOWARDS THE END OF the Ludlow contract, I got a call from Rocco offering me a job. Another local contractor in Bunbury had won a big contract for an infill sewerage job for the Water Corporation. The job was in a town called Quairading, about 160 kilometres inland from Perth. I hadn't seen the Wheatbelt region of the state before, so I jumped at the chance to go and check it out.

It was a drive-in, drive-out site and we had the choice of either sharing a motel room or camping in some old railway huts on the edge of town. I've never liked sharing rooms, so chose to camp down in the railyards. They reminded me of shearers' quarters – rough and ready with no frills – but I'd lived in rougher places and it didn't bother me. Some of the boys thought I was mad.

There was not much to see around the camp. I stood on the rickety old porch of my railway hut, surveying my surroundings. Out the front, by the edge of the highway, were rows of rusty old railway lines and old rail wagons parked up in the siding, waiting for the next wheat season.

As far as the eye could see, the fields surrounding the town were bleak and dry, burnt off by the harsh summer heat, with only wheat stubble sticking out of the ground and the odd scattering of gumtrees in the distance.

Even though I was out in the open, I felt quite claustrophobic – something I'd never felt before. I'd worked in the outback in some fairly remote areas and never felt closed in, probably because there was always something to see – whether it was wildlife or bush – to take my mind off the remoteness. But, as I stood there that day, I couldn't put my finger on why I felt so hemmed in, until I realised the empty wheatfields surrounding the town looked like a blank canvas – nothing there.

However, the place grew on me as the seasons slowly changed. The wheat farmers ploughed their fields and sowed their crops with huge, dual-wheeled Steiger tractors. The wheatfields surrounding the town slowly came to life, turning into a patchwork of green and yellow. Odd-looking ProGator tractors started appearing on the scene, ready to do the spraying.

With the approach of the hotter summer months, the area became a hive of activity, and it was interesting to watch the big John Deere headers harvesting wheat throughout the district. There were wheat trucks going back and forth constantly, tipping their loads at the wheat bins and contractors moving their big combines down the narrow country roads.

It was a real family affair: husbands, wives, sons and daughters took turns driving the big headers, tractors and trucks, working around the clock to get their crops harvested in time, before any rain.

While digging up half of Quairading, we got to know the locals. They were going to benefit from our work, getting rid of all their smelly old septic tanks and connecting their homes into a new sewer line that would flow out of town into the new wastewater treatment ponds we were also constructing.

Every morning for about eight months, I'd drive past a very stern-looking local woman, who always stood on the corner by the butcher's shop. Whenever I saw her, I would smile and give her a big, cheery wave as I rounded the corner. Without fail, she would glare back at me with a face like thunder. I was determined to get a smile out of her, so I tried a range of greetings – 'Morning,' 'Hi,' 'What a wonderful day,' 'You're looking nice today' – but I just couldn't make her smile.

A local bloke by the name of Griffo was working with us. One day, he said, 'Hey, Mick, are you coming to the big show the week after next, bro?'

'What show's that, Griffo?'

'Quairading Ag Show. It's got a bar, so how about joining me for a beer? All the mob will be there.'

That sounded like a plan to me.

The morning of the show, traffic was diverted away from the main road through town. Rows of plastic tables and chairs were set up along the street, and it slowly filled up with the locals. It was clear they were waiting for some sort of show to start.

Then I noticed a bunch of people standing in the middle of the road. Most of them were dressed in Western wear, Akubra hats and shiny cowboy boots. Next minute, they formed three rows, with a bloke wearing a big white cowboy hat out the front, and Billy Ray Cyrus's 'Achy Breaky Heart' started blasting out over the loudspeakers. They all hooked their thumbs into their belt loops and started dancing. They stepped to the side then stepped to the back, did a little kick, walked forward in a row, did a bit of gyrating, back and forth, back and forth. I'm sure it was hot stuff if you liked line dancing. I gingerly looked around and hoped that no one recognised me.

They finished their dance and I clapped politely. For their next big number, 'Boot Scootin' Boogie' started blasting over the airwaves. 'Mmm, this must be one of their favourites,' I muttered under my breath, as I heard the crowd cheering. I started to tap my foot because I didn't want to seem rude, I was hoping to blend in with the crowd while still looking over my shoulder.

Oh, wow! They all did a turn at once.

Next, 'Copperhead Road' boomed out over the town – that was more like it. The group was now walking forwards a little faster. Kick. Walk back a little faster. Kick. But wait! They added a little ankle roll this time. They'd tricked me!

'Hey, Mick,' shouted a voice from behind me. It was Griffo. 'Whatya doing watching that shit? The bar is over that way, bro!' He pointed towards the nearby footy oval.

Bugger. Sprung. Never mind. 'Yeah, be over shortly, Griffo,' I said.

Parked on one side of the road was a Mack tractor unit from a road train that caught my attention. Some burly local blokes were hooking up a long, thick tow-rope to the bumper of the truck. The boot-scooting display had finally stopped, and I could now come out of hiding from behind a street sign. I decided it looked more entertaining than the boot scooting, so I wandered over.

A crowd had formed down both sides of the truck. It was a truck-towing contest. Four blokes at a time would pull the Mack truck along to a mark on the road, and the team to get there fastest would win. Going by all the blue singlets and jelly bellies hanging over pairs of Stubbies, I reckoned most of the contestants were truckies.

After the truck-towing contest was finished and the winners had received their prize, the crowd dispersed, so I wandered up the road to the footy oval where the Ag Show was being held.

Parked out in the middle of the ground was a massive New Holland tractor with triple wheels all around. I'd thought the John Deere and Steiger tractors were big, but this tractor was huge. Mind you, the Wheatbelt region covered roughly 155,000 square kilometres up past Geraldton, inland towards Southern

Cross and right down towards Esperance. No wonder the gear was super-sized. That much land would definitely take a fair amount of ploughing and seeding.

After watching wood chopping and sheep shearing and wandering around the various stalls and farm machinery displays, it was time for a beer, so I headed for the bar.

'Cheers, Griffo,' I said, as a group of us sat around a table having a beer.

'Hey, Mick, are you staying for the live show this evening?' asked Griffo.

'Not line dancing again, Griffo?' I said, rolling my eyes.

'Nah, bro, that's why it's on in the morning. They get it over and done with, so no one has to suffer! Mind you, Mick, you looked like you were enjoying it.'

'Bugger off, Griffo,' I said, and laughed.

I looked over towards the crowd. The big, stern-looking lady I waved to each morning was staring at me. She started walking towards me.

'Oh no, I'm in trouble now,' I whispered to Griffo.

'What did you say, Mick? In trouble?'

As I turned back around, the woman was standing right beside me.

'Hey, Mick, this is my sister Sally,' said Griffo.

'Your sister, you say, Griffo?' I replied, a little shocked.

'Yeah, that's right. What? You know her or something?' he asked.

Sally smiled and we both laughed.

After a bit of small talk, she said, 'Crikey, must go. Catch you fellas later.'

Sally headed towards the stage and picked up a microphone. As the band began playing, she started to sing a country song. The voice that came from her was like the voice of an angel. It took me by surprise. I could have sat there and listened to her all night.

'Man, she can sing,' I said to Griffo.

'Yeah, she's very talented. Has a CD out with her music and everything. Does painting and carving as well.'

'Does she make didgeridoos by any chance?' I asked.

'Yeah, hundred bucks, bro. I'll ask her to make you one.'

Two weeks later, Griffo and Sally arrived at my hut to drop off my new didgeridoo. She had painted it in traditional colours, unlike the brightly painted ones I'd seen in the tourist shops. Plus, she gave me a beautiful hand-painted fridge magnet depicting a kangaroo in a bright desert sunset. The magnet's on the fridge now and I still have my prized didgeridoo.

* * *

We had worked our way down the laneways behind the Quairading shops, digging about two-and-a-half to three metres deep as we went. The 20-tonner was struggling because the ground was like concrete. Hard ground tends to kick the digger bucket all over the show. We had to chip and scrape or rock break to make any progress.

Where we were able to dig the sewer trench, it was only 600 millimetres wide, straight down, so the dozer driver had to have a good eye to keep straight and keep the machine level. If it wasn't level, by the time we reached three metres, we could be half-a-pipe-width out, which meant starting at the top again.

At knock-off time, we all shot into the local pub for a midi or two. The barmaid called herself the Queen of Quairading and she didn't like us outsiders much.

Apart from three or four local blokes, most of the boys on the job were from Bunbury, even the subbies who were building the poo ponds. To start with, it was a bit of them and us with the locals, especially the young blokes, as they were worried about their girlfriends jumping the fence. This was fair enough now that Mark had joined us.

Friday night was the night in Quairading as the rest of the week was dead. One Saturday night, I decided to wander down into town for a beer. It was about eight o'clock in the evening, and Rocco had just driven up from Bunbury to help us out for a month.

As I got closer to the pub, I could see him leaning against a streetlight.

'Gidday, Rocco. You didn't have to stand outside in the dark and wait for me, mate,' I said.

'How ya going, Mick? Yep, she's a quiet old town alright. Even the pub's quiet.'

'Oh, you been inside then?'

'Nah, not yet.'

'Then how do you know it's quiet?' I asked. 'Come on, let's go and have a beer and catch up on the goss, mate.'

'I've tried the door, Mick. It won't open.'

'Is it stuck, or something? Did you try giving it a boot?'

'I didn't have to. Read the sign on the door.' He pointed.

'Pub closed,' it read.

With the pub shut, me and the subbies made our own entertainment down at the rail camp on Saturdays. One night, I set up my CD player, which looked like an old ghetto blaster, on the kitchen bench and pulled out my '70s Greatest Hits' album, and we all got drunk.

It didn't matter how noisy the party got. We were in the middle of nowhere, on the edge of town, so there was no one to hear us. Everyone just sang away and no one cared. There were no egos.

At about midnight, one of the subbies, Rob, piped up, 'Man, I used to love dancing to this song.'

'Who cares, Rob? Get up and dance,' I urged.

'Nah, it's not the same, Mick,' he said.

'True, true. Hey, I've got an idea, back in a jiffy,' I slurred as I staggered out onto the porch.

After a bit of banging and crashing in the cupboard, I returned to the kitchen. 'Everyone, everyone! May I have your attention? This is Barbara. Barbara's a broomstick,' I slurred.

'Barbara, these are the boys. Would you like to dance, Barbara?' I asked, as I gazed at the grubby wooden handle I was holding in front of me.

'Oh yes, please, Mick,' I mimicked, in my most girly voice. And off I went, dancing around the room to hoots of laughter.

Rob got up and grabbed his rusty chrome diner chair in a loving embrace, staring meaningfully into its stained Formica back rest, then he headed off, dancing around the room to 'If You Can't Give Me Love' by Suzi Quatro.

Everyone cracked up laughing and they all started grabbing whatever they could for a partner: a bench seat, a mop, even a frying pan (clean, of course).

In the end, most of the boys up at the motel wanted to stay down at the rail camp.

* * *

One winter's afternoon, we stopped digging for the day, packed up all our gear and decided to stand around and have a beer. We were up a side street on the end of town. Most of the country towns out west had wide gravel verges with no grass and maybe the odd half-dead tree growing in them.

As we got into our second carton of beer, Mark piped up, 'Man, it's getting a bit nippy, isn't it?'

Rob, the subbie, hopped off the back off his truck and pulled down a couple of wooden pallets and we raided half of the branches from a sad-looking tree on the road verge for kindling.

Someone tipped a bit of diesel on the wood and – hey presto! – everyone was warming their hands in front of our new bonfire.

After a few more beers, we took it in turns to pinch a few more branches off the half-dead tree on the verge. We had an awesome young fella working for us called Sean. He owned a pair of cowboy stockwhips and he knew how to handle them.

'Hey, Sean, got your stockwhips handy?' I asked. 'Show us what you can do, mate.'

By that time, the boys were getting boisterous.

'Yeah, no worries, Mick,' Sean said. He headed off to his tip truck and fossicked around in the dark inside the cab for a few minutes, and came back holding two leather stockwhips.

He gave the whips a little flick as they neatly unfurled in front of him, near the crackling fire.

Speaking of which, it was Mark's turn to pinch some more branches off the half-dead tree and to scavenge the neighbourhood for firewood.

Crack! Crack! Sean waved his stockwhips around his head like a true stockman. Crack! Crack! The sound echoed out into the still winter's night like rifle fire.

'Hey, Mick, do you want a go, mate?' Sean asked.

'Bugger off! My welts are still burning,' I replied.

I called out to Rob, who was standing on the other side of the fire. 'Have a go, Rob, they're a piece of cake,' I said as I grinned into the firelight.

Speaking of fire, it was my turn to pinch some more branches off the half dead tree on the verge and scavenge the neighbourhood for firewood.

Crack! went Rob's whip. Crack!

'Aaagh!' That was the sound of Rob in pain as he hopped around the bonfire, rubbing one of his buttocks to the sound of laughter.

'You hesitated, Rob. Don't be scared of them, mate. The trick is to have no fear. It's like fending off a wild animal, mate – you gotta show them who's the boss. Crack them hard and fast and don't hesitate,' Sean said.

'Don't hesitate. Right. Don't hesitate,' said Rob, with a look of concentration, then he swung one of the stockwhips around his head with all his might like a true professional.

A loud crack echoed into the darkness to a chorus of cheers.

But Rob got a bit excited and carried away. Buoyed by his success, he swung the other stockwhip back behind his head. There was an almighty Crack! followed by 'Ah shit! Ah shit!'

By then, Rob was frantically rubbing a huge welt on the back of his neck. If you've ever been flicked by a tea towel by your nasty big brother, this would have felt about 50 times worse than that.

A local cop car pulled up with its blue lights flashing. The older copper was behind the wheel. 'Gidday, boys, having a bit of fun, are we?' he said. 'Down at the station we thought we heard firearms going off. You boys aren't misbehaving now, are you? The shots sound like they're coming from this direction.'

Sean stepped forward, 'Sorry for making a noise, officer, but we're just clowning round with my stockwhips.'

'Stockwhips? Well, give me a demo then, son,' the officer said, climbing out of the patrol car, followed by his mate.

Sean put on such a display that the coppers told him to do it one more time as they watched on in fascination.

Sean, who also happened to be a rodeo champion, made it look so easy, but he must have practised for hours.

'Well done, son,' said the older cop after the display had finished. 'Here, give me a go!'

Sean handed one of the stockwhips over to him.

'Right, son, what do I do?'

Sean talked him through it, then said to him with a grin, 'Crack it hard and fast, and you can't go wrong!'

The copper gave the stockwhip a flick and made a bit of a crack. He flicked it a bit harder the next time and it cracked a bit louder. He'd got his confidence up, so he swirled the stockwhip round his head and gave it all he had.

There was an almighty crack, followed by 'Ah! Ow! That hurts.' His voice echoed down the street as he rubbed his fat buttocks vigorously.

We were all laughing, and, like most country coppers, he saw the funny side and laughed at himself. He wished us goodnight and gingerly slid back behind the wheel of his patrol car and drove off.

The cops hadn't even batted an eyelid about us drinking at the side of the road, or our dying bonfire on the verge.

Speaking of dying on the verge, one of the boys asked, 'What are you doing over there, Mick?'

'Yeah, be there in a minute,' came my voice, out of the dark, as I yanked, pulled, huffed and puffed.

One more yank. 'Ah, got you,' I muttered, as I dragged the trunk of the dead tree over to the fire. Well, half-dead anyway, I thought, as I rolled it onto the fire.

23

Seeing the light

SUMMER ARRIVED. I WAS SHOWN a shortcut back to Bunbury, cutting inland instead of driving via Perth. It took me through miles and miles of wheatfields.

It was just after harvest time, so things had quietened down. I headed out of town one Friday afternoon in my little old Toyota Corolla sedan. It was a bit embarrassing to drive – it looked like a car your grandfather would own. However, it was a reliable car and economical on petrol, although it did have a bad habit of burning more oil than petrol. That was the reason for all the empty oil containers lying scattered on the floor in the back of the car.

After a few kilometres of driving through burnt, dry, wheatfields, the narrow country road rose up onto a narrow causeway where I passed a sign that read 'Floodway'. As I drove along, I had a beautiful, panoramic view of a huge, dry salt lake spread out as far as the eye could see.

Halfway along the causeway was another sign. This one said 'Ford'. The road dropped down onto a concrete pad, then rose up again onto the causeway. Yeah right, this place was so barren and dry, how could it possibly flood?

The causeway gradually widened back out to a proper road width again, the salt lake disappeared in my rear-view mirror, and it was back to barren wheatfields again. Over to the south-west, the horizon was jet-black. It looked like a storm was brewing.

Apart from the odd stretch of driving on the main road, all I saw were wheatfields until I got all excited when I spotted a wheat bin in the distance near Pingelly, which provided a welcome change of scenery.

As I headed south towards Narrogin, the rain got heavier and the storm got closer as it approached from the west. Suddenly there were loud crashes of thunder and a violent forked lightning display as I headed on into the storm. I had the driver's window down because the day was still stinking hot and muggy. The old Toyota had no air-con.

Bang! went the thunder again. Crack! went the forked lightning as it flashed nearby, followed by rattling rolls of thunder. I had never heard or seen such a display of thunder and lightning before.

The window wipers on the old Toyota weren't the greatest, so – with limited visibility – I crawled along slowly while the rain bucketed down. My nose was just about touching the windscreen as I tried to see where I was going.

The sky had gone dark within the storm, so I flicked my headlights on. A deafening clap of thunder sounded right above me, accompanied by a loud cracking sound, and a blinding white light flashed within inches of my driver's side window. For a split second, the car was bathed in a glaring light so bright that it left me blinded for a moment or two. I shook my head, trying to shift the pink stars dancing around in my vision while also trying to stay on the road.

'Man, that was lucky,' I said out loud. 'Stuff this! I nearly got fried.'

I accelerated off as I fought to get out of the eye of the storm.

Just before Narrogin, about 150 kilometres south of Quairading, it was time to top up with engine oil.

After I'd fed the thirsty Corolla, I threw another empty oil container over my shoulder into the back of the car, then headed on through Williams towards Collie before darkness fell. The road from Williams to Bunbury runs through several state forests, and it was crawling with roos.

Finally, just after sunset, the little Corolla made its way home into Bunbury.

On Saturday night, I caught up with Rocco for a drink at the Highway Hotel and got talking about Quairading.

'Yeah, Mick, at least the pubs stay open after eight o'clock here!' Rocco laughed before adding, 'And you don't have to put up with a bunch of sweaty ag contractors ogling the barmaid in desperation because there's nothing else to look at in the bar.'

'Hey, Rocco, do you know the barmaid up there calls herself the Queen of Quairading?'

He almost choked on his beer. 'Queen of Quairading? Yeah, right.'

After spending the weekend in Bunbury, I headed back to Quairading on Sunday night. I took the same route, but this time most of the trip was in the dark.

Travelling inland, I only saw one or two other vehicles on the road. The further I got into the Wheatbelt, the less chance there was of seeing any other traffic. It felt like I was heading towards the ends of the earth and that I was the only person left alive. The headlights lit up nothing but wheat stubble and insects.

On the horizon, towards the north-east – where I was heading – another storm was brewing, but it was miles away. I pulled over on the side of the road to polish off my last cold Big Mac and watch nature's raw display of energy. I turned the motor off to the sound of silence – only chirping crickets keeping me company in the middle of nowhere, while I watched my own private light show.

After a wee while, I decided it was time to carry on. I bunged a bit more oil into the old Corolla, then pulled back out onto the narrow country road. Mile after mile of nothingness rolled by. Every now and then, in the distance, I could see the faint lights of a homestead twinkling in the darkness – a family, probably, tucked up watching TV. Lucky folk, I thought.

I turned off on to the last leg of the journey back to Quairading via the salt lakes. Having driven up and down the road so many times, I knew it like the back of my hand. As I sped up towards the 'Ford' sign, I knew I could take the dip at around 70 or 80 kilometres an hour, before dropping down, crossing the ford and heading back up the other side onto the causeway. In all the times I'd crossed the ford, it had always been dry.

As I approached the ford, my headlights, which were not much better than candles, lit the shiny road surface ahead. Being half asleep at the wheel, the change in surface didn't register with me. Zoom! Down I dropped into the ford.

Whoosh! A wall of water washed up over my bonnet and I went from doing 80 kilometres an hour down to zero in a matter of seconds, just about head-butting the steering wheel in the process.

The poor old Corolla gave a cough and a splutter as I made it up the other side and back on to the causeway. 'Shit, that was lucky,' I muttered. My eyes were now wide as saucers.

I passed the 'Floodway' sign and noticed my headlights light up the same shining surface on the road in front of me again. This time, I made sure I crawled at a snail's pace. As I pulled up, the shiny surface was flowing over the top of the causeway – for about 100 metres, by the look of it. With my poor headlights, it was a bit hard to judge.

I had two questions that needed answers. First, how deep was the water flowing over the causeway? Second, had the floodwater washed out any of the causeway?

'Well, only one way to find out,' I said to myself, as I climbed out into the blackness.

After a big stretch and a yawn, I kicked off my thongs. 'This is going to be interesting. I hope there's no snakes around,' I muttered, as I gingerly felt my way out through the flowing, oily shadow shining in the night sky. Step by step, I made my way slowly, feeling the road beneath my toes.

Bump. 'Eugh, what the hell was that?'

Something slithered past my foot. 'Ah shit, what was that?' I cried.

I was on my tiptoes, trying to peer down into the dark, oily flow. Metre by metre, I kept going.

'Cool, the road's still there,' I whispered to myself in relief.

I shuffled my way out into the middle of the causeway. 'Ah! Ah! What's that bloody crawling up my leg?' I yelled. I was just about beside myself.

It turned out to be a large beetle, which I swatted off my leg and back into the water.

By then I had got a sweat up, which was a signal to the mozzies and they came out in force.

Buzz buzz … slap! 'Little sods.'

I slapped the back of my neck and nearly tripped over. Stuff it, I'd had enough.

The water was just below my knees at its deepest point. I decided that if the road was washed out further along, then so be it.

'The car's had its day, anyway,' I muttered, as I swatted away another mozzie.

I felt my way back to the car, then stood beside my tyres and tried to gauge the depth of the water to see if the car was high enough to drive on through, without drowning the engine.

Yeah, near enough, I decided. As long as I kept moving and kept a bow wave up if it got too deep, we should be hunky dory.

I climbed back into the car and edged my way into the flow, quietly puttering along. Halfway across, I held my breath for the next bit, hoping the road was still there. Otherwise, it was going to be a long walk home.

With a sigh of relief, I made it out the other side of the causeway, thankful that the car hadn't floated off back to Perth.

Finally, I spotted the flickering lights of Quairading in the distance. I drove past the giant wheat bins, then turned off into the rail camp at about midnight. I was pleased that my marathon trip was finally over. Once again, the mighty Corolla had survived another trip.

* * *

The Quairading job was coming to an end, with the sewer pipes laid, poo ponds dug and plastic-lined manholes finished. All we had left to do were the footpaths, kerbs and driveways to pour and verges to reinstate. We thought they would be a breeze after finishing the major jobs.

One morning, we backed a truck up to pour some concrete for a driveway crossing and the kerbs we had ripped out. Because there were gravel verges, the locals could drive around the newly poured road crossing and into their driveways.

I banged on the door of one house to let them know what we were doing and was greeted by a mob of little kids. Dad came out onto the porch, and I explained to him that he could still drive around the wet concrete into his property and that we'd just placed witches' hats around the crossing to cone it off and stop anyone using it.

While we waited for the concrete to go off so we could screed it, we headed to the next street over to pour a footpath that was already formed up and ready to go. Once that was done, we moved a couple of streets over to where another concrete truck was waiting on site for us. We poured another road crossing, then I shot back to the shipping container we used for storage to look for another trowel.

My route to the container took me back past the crossing we had poured earlier. There, I noticed the witches' hats all around the newly poured driveway crossing had been bowled over.

'Oh no, that doesn't look good,' I said, as I pulled over.

There were two tyre ruts straight through the middle of the driveway. I glanced over at the newly poured kerb and could see some little finger marks in it. These kids hadn't scratched their names into the concrete, which is easy to repair. Instead, they'd scooped out handfuls of concrete and thrown it everywhere.

Suspecting the worst, I headed over to the next street to find a similar scene in our newly poured footpath. It had names scratched into it and footprints in it.

I drove back to let the boys know what had happened. There wasn't much we could do with the driveway crossing as the concrete had gone off. The boys patched the kerbs the best they could, but the finish looked rough.

Even after we had gone back and repaired the damage, the kids came out and made a mess of the concrete. The boss was fuming. This time, he told us not to repair any of the concrete and just let it harden.

The following morning, as we went through and checked the job, Mark was laughing at the two big ruts in the driveway and the chunks out of the kerbs. It looked rough as guts with footprints all through it – and that's the way it stayed. The shire didn't make us rip it out.

Not long before the infill sewerage job was finished, I drove back to Bunbury for the weekend, without incident. One of the subcontractors we had worked with in the Wheatbelt was looking for a digger operator to drive their near-new 28-tonne

Samsung digger. I decided to apply for the job, so I popped into their yard just out of Bunbury to say hi.

I wandered over to their office and stood at the reception counter. I glanced over at a row of desks, and said 'Gidday' to the owner's son, Richie, who had been working up in the Wheatbelt with us.

A couple of middle-aged ladies looked up from their desks and gave me a smile. They were doing a bit of admin, by the looks of things. Another woman had her back to me. Then she spun around on her office chair to face me. I could tell that she recognised me straight away, by her snooty, pouting pose and a 'Just look at me', 'CAT's got the cream', 'I've finally made it' sort of expression on her face.

'How can I help you, sir?' she asked as she stuck a pen in the corner of her mouth and raised an eyebrow.

'Well, well, well, I'll be blowed! If it isn't the Queen of Quairading! How about a couple of midis of super, thanks, love?'

She shot me a filthy look and the ladies behind her laughed their heads off. Even Richie's old man, who was in his office behind me, cracked up laughing.

'Hey, is that you out there, Mick? Come on in for a chat, mate,' he called out.

24

A bad taste in your mouth

I STARTED MY NEXT job on my near-new Samsung digger. The company was subcontracting to a crowd from Perth, and I had been warned that the boss running the show was a hard man who had booted a few of the operators off site for not performing. Now, where had I heard that before?

The job had just about finished, but I was hired to help dig the last bit of a CLS or concrete-lined steel pipeline up a steep hill in a bush reserve. This was in the Eaton–Australind area of Bunbury. The pipelayer, Merv, was in his late thirties and built like the Incredible Hulk. Apparently, he'd spent some time working as a stripper in a touring show. Because it was summer, all he wore were boots, a hard hat, short shorts and a fluoro singlet, which was straining at the seams. I don't know if that was same outfit he wore when he was stripping – either way, he looked like a stripper.

Merv didn't speak much, possibly because his vocal cords had been stuffed by steroids in his younger days. When I spoke to him, he answered in a quiet little squeaky voice.

'What's that, Merv? Can't hear you, mate. Speak a little louder,' I'd frequently have to ask. It used to wind him up.

There was something odd about a voice like that coming from a man with his build. I had to try hard to keep a straight face and not embarrass him.

I cleared a path through the trees up the hill, ready for the pipeline, then started to box out a section of the hill so I could reach the bottom of the trench. Being all sand, it was fairly quick to dig out. I excavated for about 12 metres then I dug out a bell hole to allow room for the welder to wriggle under the pipes to weld and wrap them. The steel pipes were craned in with the digger.

As we worked, Merv would set up a laser level to give us our depths. When we were down about five or six metres deep, I battered the sides of the trench right back to take the weight off them so that we didn't get buried alive.

Merv had a sixth sense about when he was needed. He would sit down by the last bell hole on an upturned plastic bucket and nod off to sleep while I dug the next section. Then, just as I was about to dig out the last bucketful of sand, his head would spring up and he would wander up the trench with his measuring tape, ready to mark out the next bell hole.

One morning, we were getting our gear out of the sea container, when a white Land Cruiser pulled up on the job. 'It's the boss. What's he want?' whispered Merv.

The boss and another bloke climbed out of the ute and started walking towards us. This was the first time I'd seen the superintendent on this job, but he sure looked familiar.

'Mr Bellamy, how are we this fine morning?' he asked. It was the bloody Belgian.

'Always the epitome of health, thanks, Van,' I replied as we shook hands.

He introduced me to his foreman. 'This is Mick. Now, Mick and I have been in a few campaigns together. Then again, we've fought a few battles as well.'

We both started laughing.

Van left us alone on that job. Better the devil you know.

By the time Merv and I got halfway up the hill, a welding contractor, Phil, had turned up on site, towing his diesel generator. Merv knew what was in store, so said to me in his quiet voice, 'Mick, you can be his TA for the day. I've got a small job to finish down the road.'

The TA or trade assistant's job is basically to run around after the welder. As welders go, Phil wasn't a bad bloke – unlike some other welders I've met, who acted like prima donnas.

My job was to run the leads down into the bell hole then clamber back down the slope with the welding rods and angle grinder. As Phil was welding, he would stop from time to time and I would pass him another welding rod.

After he had finished welding, he would grind the weld smooth himself then wrap the pipe with special tape. Once, while he was grinding away, I looked up and saw flames. One of the sparks from the angle grinder must have set the reserve on fire, even though we were five metres down in the hole.

Being a typical welder, Phil just looked at me and said, 'You're the TA. Go and put it out, Mick.'

He wanted me to crank up the digger and try to put the fire out. I pointed out that it was a waste of time as the fire was already racing off towards some houses by then. Instead, I ran up the bank to see what I could do.

I was surprised at how fast the fire had spread through the reserve with only a small breeze behind it. I'd hate to think what damage the fire could have done if it had been a windy day.

Luckily, there was a fire break around the edge of the reserve, and it did its job. I was surprised at how fast the volunteer fire brigade turned up. It was a credit to them. Phil got told off, but by that time he was just finishing the last wrap on the pipe.

The following morning, Merv came back and we finished digging up the hill, stopping short of the reservoir. Our plan was to move the existing sewer line out of the way, lay our steel pipe, then reconnect the existing sewer line back across our new steel pipe.

The owners of the two houses were given a Portaloo each and told not to use their toilets or flush them, and – all going well – we would have their sewer pipe reconnected after lunch. The Water Corporation even shouted the homeowners out to a free lunch while we dug up the pipes.

I dug around the sewer pipe, and Franco, a Watercorp contractor, cut through the old sewer pipe with a handsaw, then placed a rubber bung up the pipe. With that done, he left us to dig through and lay the steel pipe. We had a good run and laid our pipe, and as soon as we were finished, we phoned Franco to let him know.

By the time Franco returned to reconnect the sewer pipe, we had made a big hole for him to stand in. He was standing on top of our new steel pipe at eye level with the old sewer pipe that was protruding out of the bank.

Merv quietly asked Franco if it was a good idea to stand in front of the sewer pipe.

'Whaddaya mean? The line will be empty. We've given them Portaloos for that reason,' Franco responded with confidence.

'Okay,' whispered Merv as he moved quietly away.

Franco had to stick his arm all the way up the sewer pipe to undo the wingnut on the rubber bung. Then he slid the bung back down the pipe to free it. Just as he pulled the bung out of the pipe – whoosh! – out came someone's sneaky number two, with the rest of the contents of their loo, straight into Franco's face.

We all started gagging and Merv was on the verge of heaving.

Franco tried to put on a bit of bravado. 'You bunch of fluffs. What's wrong with a bit of sewage in your mouth?' he said, as he attempted to spit out a bit of toilet paper. His face reminded me of a two-year old's after he'd just eaten a yummy piece of chocolate cake.

The Belgian walked up to my digger the following morning. 'Hey, Mick, what are they paying you, if you don't mind me asking?' he said.

'Not a lot, mate,' I replied, giving him a figure.

'Really? Look, how about coming over to us, say, just after Christmas? There's only a month to go, so pull the pin just before Christmas so it doesn't look so obvious that we've poached you.'

25

Digging up Donnybrook

VAN KEPT HIS WORD and got me a start with his company early in 2000. One of my first jobs for them involved working with Merv on a new subdivision up at Karratha, in the Pilbara region of Western Australia, about 1500 kilometres north of Perth.

The Pilbara was an eye-opener. It looked nothing like the other parts of the state that I'd worked in or visited. I felt like I'd landed on Mars – everything was red – red Pindan sand, red clay, even the rocky hills behind the town were red. When I first looked up at those hills, I assumed they were old waste dumps and that the rocks had been dumped there – but they just looked that way naturally.

Set in its red backdrop, the Karratha township looked like an oasis with its lush green palm trees and nicely kept gardens. The sunsets were magic the way they lit up the red rock on the hills, which towered over the town like a beacon, while the sun dropped down beneath the flaming horizon. The place had its own rugged beauty.

Speaking of rugged beauty, Merv – as usual dressed only in short shorts and straining fluoro vest – was down in his trench packing around a water main, which we were laying near the edge of the old road. Meanwhile, I was chipping and scraping, as the ground was like concrete, when a car pulled over and a nice-looking young woman hopped out.

With her nose in the air, she totally ignored me as she leaned over the trench and, without a word, handed Merv a piece of paper. Then she hopped back in her car and drove off without waiting for a response.

Puzzled, I stopped the digger and asked Merv what that was all about.

'Oh, I get that all the time,' he said.

'Get what all the time?'

'Chicks' phone numbers,' he said as he screwed the note up in a ball and threw it over his shoulder.

'Man, I've never had that happen to me, ever.'

Merv was the only bloke I knew who could lay pipe all day out in sweltering 40-degree heat with only short shorts, sleeveless vest and a hard hat. It was a wonder he didn't get cooked.

Down in the trench one day, Merv's steel shovel fell over. When he reached over to pick it up, he leaned over a little bit too far, and his hulking, muscle-bound frame toppled him over like a log.

'Timber!' I yelled, but Merv didn't have much of a sense of

humour as he flailed on the ground like an upturned beetle, stuck on this back in the narrow trench.

I couldn't help laughing, he looked so ridiculous.

'You think that's funny, Mick?' said Merv as he finally managed to roll onto his hands and knees.

'Sorry for laughing, Merv. Do you want me to brush the sand off your back, mate?'

'Bugger off, Mick,' he squeaked, feeling around for his shovel.

That was probably the most Merv had ever spoken to me in a single day.

* * *

My next job was in Donnybrook, just south of Bunbury, where the company had a depot. Donnybrook is the heart of Western Australia's main apple-growing region and the countryside around it is green and picturesque. When we drove into Donnybrook itself, it was a different story.

The South Western Highway cut straight through the middle of town. There was a shortage of car parks on the same side of the highway as the shops, so the locals used to park in a big, open water table drain on the other side of the highway. From there, they would have to dodge the trucks and cars flying through the town to cross over to the shops or the pub.

Getting home from the pub was also a problem because you risked getting run over a second time. If you managed to get across in one piece, you then faced the tricky task of backing your car out onto the other side of the highway, which was just as dangerous!

Apart from a rundown railway station and a bit of a park with a band rotunda in the middle of it, the main feature of the town was some nice, old oak trees. The one thing about Donnybrook that I really liked was its giant Granny Smith apple streetlights, but even they were faded and falling to bits. At the far end of town was a big apple-packing shed that had mountains of old apple crates stacked out on the grass beside the railway line.

Needless to say, the town was crying out for a makeover – and that's why we were there. Our contract was to streetscape the whole shopping precinct and lay new sewer and stormwater mains around it. It was a big job and our crowd had hired another drainage company to give us a hand.

Our supervisor, Snowy, was probably in his late fifties. He was old school – called a spade a spade. He worked hard and played hard. He was also the spitting image of Albert Steptoe from the TV comedy *Steptoe and Sons*. Unfortunately, Snowy had emphysema, so he would get into coughing fits occasionally. When this happened, his face would go lobster-red and he would start to choke, then his tongue would stick out. But it passed quickly enough.

Snowy drove me around the back of the shops, below which was the Preston River. 'See all those wet spots leaching down the bank into the river?' he said.

'What are they? Springs or something?'

'You wouldn't want to swim in that river, mate. It's waste water from all the septic tanks and leach drains from behind the shops,' he said, nodding his head. 'That's one of our first jobs: building a new sewer line out to the poo ponds to stop the pollution that's been leaching into the river for decades.'

I drove an old 14-tonne Sumitomo zero-swing digger. Digging through the old leach drains in the middle of summer wasn't the greatest job, because the stink was horrendous. Working with me were our two drainers, Jessie and Tim. Jessie was a big bloke and Tim was a small, slim fella with half his front teeth missing. They had been knocked out by a big rubber ring he was trying to put on the end of a pipe one day.

Once the sewer line was hooked up to the shops, we had to go back and dig out the old septic tanks, which oozed out slimy black muck, even after they were pumped out. The next job was laying the new stormwater lines. The old road layout was going to be changed, with two car-parking areas being added across the road, so we were tasked with linking the new stormwater lines to the single main line. This line passed between the old Railway Hotel, down a laneway and into a concrete chamber where all the rubbish was filtered out before the water was discharged into the Preston River.

I had just finished laying a concrete stormwater pipe in the laneway beside the pub. Tim was busy down in the trench packing blue metal around his pipe. Dug into the ground above his head was his long steel crowbar, which he used for pushing the pipes home. When crowbars weren't being used, the tips of them would always be speared into the ground to stand them up. If a crowbar was laid flat on the ground, it would cook in the sun and fry the hands of anyone who tried to use it. But leave it upright and it would stay cool.

Meanwhile, Lynchie pulled up in his nice new CAT 950-wheel loader. He was a tall, slim guy with curly dark hair, and always seemed to have a rollie sticking out the corner of his mouth. He walked over to Tim and leaned over the trench to ask him about something. Tim looked up to answer him. The top of Tim's head was just sticking out above the trench and, as usual, he wasn't wearing his hard hat.

Lynchie leaned against Tim's big steel crowbar to itch his shoulder. Almost in slow motion, I saw the heavy steel crowbar topple straight over, across the trench then smack poor Tim's noggin. The only reason it didn't split his head in half was because the crowbar hit the other side of the trench.

Tim staggered around in circles, no doubt seeing bright-coloured stars, with a huge gash across his scalp. In typical fashion, in between fits of coughing, Snowy told him not to mess around at the doctor's and to come straight back to work.

I know what I would have told Snowy if it had been me on the receiving end of that crowbar!

A couple of hours later, Tim was back down in his trench. We all queued up to have a look at the hospital's handiwork. All the doctor had done was put a few rows of staples in his scalp, which made him look as if he had a zipper in his head. They hadn't even bothered to shave his head or dress his wound.

Finally, with all the stormwater pipes laid, it was time to set up some temporary traffic lights so that we could dig out one half of the highway, backfill it with a metre of limestone, seal the new section, then switch the traffic to the other side and start again on the other side of the road.

I was sitting down in the park with the boys one lunchtime when I decided to go and buy some fruit to help improve public relations. By that stage, the shopkeepers had taken turns to yell at us, mainly because, along with the road, most of their shop fronts were missing.

I wandered into a fruit and veggie shop and recognised the owner stacking cucumbers over in one corner. She was forever swearing at us, mainly because Lynchie had pushed all her apple crates into a pile with his loader, turning them into kindling wood. To be fair, this only happened after she had been asked then warned by Snowy countless times to move them. The crates were on public land, where we needed to start the new car park.

I glanced around the shop and, in a dark corner, spotted the side profile of a bloke standing at the till, who looked like he needed a shave quite badly. His arms appeared to be quite hairy as well, but it was a bit hard to tell in the dim light.

I put some juicy plums into a bag and grabbed a couple of delicious-looking Granny Smiths, then wandered over to the till. 'How's your day going, mate?' I asked.

The person behind the counter turned to face me and, to my shock and embarrassment, she snapped: 'That'll be five dollars, mate.'

* * *

That afternoon, our HR manager arrived on site.

'What's he want?' I asked Merv, who was back from the Pilbara and giving us a hand.

'Oh no, work reviews,' he moaned.

Me, Merv and Lynchie got a message asking us to head over to Snowy's office for our work reviews. Basically, they're like a school report. Two bosses have to write about you over the year, whether you've misbehaved at work and been a naughty boy, or if you've excelled yourself and crawled up the bosses' backsides.

Craig, the HR manager, poked his head out of the office door: 'Right, Merv, you're first. Come on in, mate.'

Sitting in the corner of the office was Snowy, who also had to attend the reviews.

As we waited there, Lynchie and I heard Merv going off.

Five minutes later, I heard him say, 'Right, have you finished with me? Can I go now?'

Out of the office stormed Merv's big, hulking frame. The wall shuddered as he slammed the door behind him, shouting, 'What a load of bullshit.'

Craig popped his head back out the door, looking a bit flustered. He was a company man, very passionate about his job. 'Okay, Mick, your turn. Come in please,' he said.

'Gidday Snowy,' I said as I took a seat.

'Right, Mick,' said Craig calmly, 'I'll explain what this is all about. Over the year, we review your work and get two supervisors' opinions so there's no personality clashes, just to let you know how you're going. For example, your strengths and weaknesses – maybe if you need further training, etcetera. Zac, your supervisor up in Karratha, has given you a glowing review.'

Snowy was squirming in his chair and I knew what that was about. We had done a rail job together up at Coolgardie where his son, Trent, had worked with us for a time. We had been widening drains down in the bottom of a rail cutting.

Trent had been spotting for me, standing by my bucket down the bottom by the rail track while I had the 45-tonne digger up on top of the cutting. For some reason, Trent thought he could talk to the boys like they were idiots and get away with it because he was Snowy's son. We didn't get off to a good start.

'Down!' he would yell over the radio.

'Out!' he would order.

To begin with, I thought he just wasn't a morning person and let it slide, but he carried on throughout the morning.

For a couple of hours, I let him get away with it, but the last straw was when I caught him shaking his head.

It was like a red rag to a bull for me, so I booted the door of the digger open and slid down over the side of the rail cutting to teach him a lesson in manners. I went sailing down the bank and we had a bit of a set-to beside the rail lines. Unbeknown to me, a rail inspector had turned up and was standing above me on the opposite side of the rail cutting. Unfortunately, all he saw was the naughty digger driver sliding down the bank about to throttle the spotter.

Anyway, Craig was flicking through some papers on the desk in Snowy's office, looking like he was readying himself to read a eulogy.

'Right.' Craig cleared his throat and, after a hint of a pause, continued. 'There's just one area where there seems to be a problem, Mick.'

'Okay, you just finished telling me I had a glowing report. Now you say there's a problem.'

He started to look a little bit uncomfortable. 'Well, the problem, it says here, is that you are short-fused,' he said a little sheepishly.

'Short-fused? Pig's arse. If that's all you've got to say, why bother?'

I looked Snowy straight in the face and said, 'I haven't had a day off all year, haven't broken a service at all on this job. I've exposed all your asbestos water mains and dug round all your power cables. I haven't damaged any property, and all you can come up with is that I'm short-fused. I'm not short-fused, pal. I just don't bloody suffer fools.'

I pointed my finger at Snowy and went on: 'Just because you're sulking over your smart-arsed son. Maybe my only weakness, as you blokes put it, is that I didn't throw the hand-held radio hard enough at him when he was sprinting down the railway line. And as for training, as you blokes call it, maybe you could teach me to run a little faster so I can catch him next time. Merv was right. This review is a waste of time.'

I stood up and Snowy pushed his head back in his chair, thinking I was going to clock him, which I wouldn't have. I quite liked the old goat.

Craig was all choked up and about to cry as I stormed out and slammed the door on the way.

Poor Lynchie looked up from rolling a smoke: 'Man, what are they saying in there, Mick? I'm too nervous to set foot in there now!'

26
Spit and polish

FROM TIME TO TIME over winter, I did a few days' work for a bloke who owned a contracting company. Jack would drive down from Perth in his Holden Statesman and show me what he wanted done on his 100-hectare lifestyle block in the Ferguson Valley area, just out of Bunbury. Most of the land was quite hilly and a lot of it was in native timber. Jack wanted the scrappy-looking trees thinned out to form nice parkland areas of grass fields with pockets of jarrah trees. He drove his Statesman around the farm like it was a Land Rover and expected me to follow him in my new Ford Falcon.

Bang … scrape … bounce … clunk … bang! I dropped into a hole that was covered in long grass as I drove through a paddock after him.

The steering rack on my near-new car was now bent, which also stuffed the alignment on the tyres. Jack didn't offer to pay for the damage. Instead, he just showed me what he wanted me to do, gave me a list of jobs, then headed back to Perth.

A near-new 20-tonne Hitachi digger had been dropped off at the property for me, so I started thinning out trees and stacking them into piles. As I worked, I got some nice glimpses out through the trees to the picturesque valley below.

I had just finished digging around the stump of a red gum to loosen it, then I reached up as high as I could with the rock bucket. Suddenly, the one-tonne bucket dropped off the quick hitch, bounced off the tree trunk and came sailing down towards me, only just missing my cab. Man, it gave me a fright. It was one of those moments when I could hear my heart beating.

I thought I must have forgotten to put the quick-hitch pin in. The quick hitch is the jaw that opens and closes over the two bucket pins. Once the jaw is closed, you have to manually slide the quick-hitch pin (basically a thin metal rod) through one hole in the quick hitch, which would slide behind the metal jaw so it couldn't open by mistake if you were to bump the switch for the quick hitch in the cab. With wedge lock couplers nowadays, they are a thing of the past.

Still shaking, I climbed out of the cab to have a look. I was surprised to find the quick-hitch pin locked in. There was no way the jaw could have opened and dropped the bucket. Shit, I mustn't have coupled it properly, I thought. That was the only thing I could put it down to. I'd have to be more careful next time, or I could wind up dropping a rock bucket into my lap.

I hitched up the bucket, put the quick-hitch pin back in, double checked it – yep, all good – then swung the rock bucket full reach to carry on bowling the red gum.

Next moment, a steel blur shot past my windscreen and thumped into the ground in a cloud of dust. My rock bucket had fallen off again!

I was fizzing. The bloody digger was trying to kill me.

Straight away, I got on the phone to Jack in Perth: 'Your bloody digger's tried to kill me twice. The bucket keeps falling off.'

'What do you mean the bucket keeps falling off? It's a new machine! Haven't you put the quick-hitch pin in?'

'Course I have. Didn't come down in the last shower, mate.'

'Well, it can't come off. It's impossible,' he said.

'Are you saying I'm a liar, mate? The jaw was closed and the quick-hitch pin was in. Your useless bucket bypassed it somehow and fell off – twice!' I yelled.

'Right, I don't know why this is happening. You're doing something wrong. I'll talk to the fitters,' Jack said, then hung up.

Ten minutes later, I got a phone call. 'Yeah, Mick, it's John from the workshop. Look, sorry, mate, the boys have put the wrong-sized quick hitch on your digger. It was a second-hand one off a 25-tonner we had in the yard. What we'll do is send a welder out to weld a bit of steel plate over the jaw so it won't happen again.'

About two hours later, a welder from Bridgetown called Tommo arrived towing a big generator behind his Land Cruiser. I think he wanted to make an impression so he'd get more work from Jack.

He had a look at the quick hitch. 'Right, Mick, I'll have to bash this pin out so I can get at the hydraulic ram that pushes the steel tongue over the pin,' he said as he started work. 'Here, hold the steel rod against the pin and I'll whack it out. Don't worry, I'm good with the sledgehammer.'

Gingerly, I held the steel rod against the pin while Mr Confidence lifted his big sledgehammer, did a couple of dummy runs, then swung it.

Swing. Bang! Swing. Bang! Swing. Bang!

My arms and hands got jarred with every blow.

'It's moving,' he gasped.

Swing. Bang! Swing. Whack!

'Ow!' He'd just clobbered my hand with the sledgehammer.

I picked off the skin smeared over my raw knuckles and, five minutes later, we tried again.

Once the hydraulic hoses were disconnected, Tommo opened up the ram, which pushes the steel tongue open and closed, by levering it open with a crowbar. Hydraulic oil spewed out onto the ground. The steel tongue slid back into the ram.

'Good, that's open far enough. Now I can weld more length onto the steel tongue,' he explained.

'You sure that ram is all the way back, Tommo? It doesn't look it.'

'Yeah, that's plenty for what we want,' he replied, then he flipped his welding mask down.

I looked away from the blue flame as sparks flew everywhere.

Once the plate was welded and the bucket was back on, Tommo assured me, 'Your bucket will never come off in a million years. You're in good hands.'

'Good hands? I know how my hands are feeling at the moment …' I muttered, as he drove off down the gravelly track.

Instead of going straight back to work, I decided to sit in peace and quiet in the forest, eat my lunch and listen to the kookaburras.

After lunch, I walked the digger back down into the gully to continue where I'd left off. I lifted my bucket high into the air to start pushing the red gum. Thump!

Another cloud of dust swirled up in front of the cab. When it cleared, there was my bucket! Tommo hadn't pushed the ram back in far enough when he'd welded on the new plate. A million years? Yeah, right, good one.

After another phone call to Jack, Tommo came back and sorted it out, after which, the bucket stayed on the digger. Even so, I wasn't happy. But, at the end of the day, they shouldn't have had to bodgy up a part that wasn't for that machine. It was bloody dangerous. I didn't even get an apology from management.

Six months after the digger had just about killed me, I went back to Jack's property to do a bit more tree thinning. It was a foggy morning when I got there, and the view below me looked very peaceful with the fog lying softly over the valleys.

I wound my way down the snaking gravel driveway and parked my car up by the toilet and shower block Jack had built for his family for when they would camp there. I grabbed my lunch bag, threw it into the cab of the digger and disappeared down the back of the farm.

I spent the day bowling trees and, at knock-off time, walked the 20-tonner back up the ridgeline onto a flat area and parked it up for the night. After being cooped up in the machine all day, I decided to walk the rest of the way back to my car.

I walked through the jarrah forest and emerged onto the grassy field surrounding the toilet block only to find a herd of dairy cows standing around my car. Where had they come from? Jack had never had any stock on his property before – well, that I'd noticed anyway.

From a distance, the metallic paintwork on my car looked pale and dull. Must've been the way the sun was shining on it, I thought. But what was that cow doing, itching its head on my bonnet? Why were those cows licking my car? The cows didn't seem to mind my presence. They just carried on with what they were doing.

As I got closer, my heart sank. When I'd left it that morning, my beloved, two-year-old, mint condition Ford Falcon Futura didn't have a single scratch on it. Now, though, my nice, shiny, red car was covered in snot and slobber. The whole car looked like a giant piece of snot, which in itself wouldn't have been a problem as I could easily wash off the drool and slobber. However, making matters much worse, the cows had rubbed themselves all over my car, trying to scratch their itches. They all had ear tags, which had scratched the panel work right round the whole car. The paint was a write-off.

I just stood there staring at my car in disbelief and the cows stood there too, staring at me with their innocent faces, big eyes and long eyelashes, tails flicking away, none the wiser. One even tried to lick my hand.

I took one more look at the car and cracked up laughing. What could I do? Nothing. What was done was done and that's all there was to it.

What I was worried about, though, was how embarrassing my drive back to Bunbury was going to be with my car looking like a lump of mucus on four wheels.

I rang up Jack. It turned out the cows were from the farm next door, which belonged to his brother.

'What? You should have parked your car behind the electric fence, Mick. That's what it's for.'

'I've never parked behind that electric fence. It's never worked as far as I know,' I said.

'Well, it's your fault, Mick.'

'No, it's not. You've never had stock on this property since I've been there.'

'Well, surely you spotted the cows while you were coming down the driveway ...'

'There was heavy fog this morning, covering all the low-lying areas. I never saw a thing,' I said. 'They were probably sheltering down in one of the gullies.'

'All right, since it's half your fault, I'll pay for half the damage to your car,' Jack offered.

'My insurance excess is 500 bucks,' I said.

'Good. Well, I'll pay 250 then.' He didn't even offer to claim it on his insurance. It would have been change in his ashtray, as he was a millionaire – but I suppose that's how he became one.

The next morning, I parked my nice, shiny but badly scratched car on the inside of the electric fence. Then I wandered back through the forest to where I'd left my digger. My job that day was to stack up all the logs I'd bowled over the previous day. I didn't have a log grapple on the machine, so I had to be a bit careful.

All was going fine. Using my bucket, I would scoop up a felled tree near the stump end, carry it over to the log pile and roll the stump end up and onto the stack, then move to the other end and push the head of the tree onto the stack.

Some of the logs were dead jarrah trees and, being a hardwood, they were very heavy. Although most of the jarrah tree stumps had rotted away, the roots that were still in the ground could be 30-centimetres around, so when I pushed one over the whole stump was gnarly and spiky, like a jagged star.

I would scoop up a jarrah tree at the base of the stump and lift it over to the log stockpile. This took a bit of yanking and pulling, and, as I moved them, some jagged bits of the stump would stick high up into the air like crooked fingers above the digger cab.

After stacking three old jarrah trees on top of the pile, I started to tidy the dead branches lying around by, scraping them into piles ready to be carted over to the log pile. I reversed my rock bucket so I could use it like a face shovel to scoop up the big piles of branches that were heaped up in the gully. Jack was keen to make a big bonfire out of the log pile once the timber had dried out.

Just before knock-off time, I threw the last pile of broken-off branches onto the stack, then started tidying up the base of the log pile. My cab door was closed to keep all the dust out.

I stopped for a drink right beside the stump end of the log pile. As I was reaching behind the seat for my drink bottle, the digger gave a shudder and a shower of smashed glass went flying round my head.

I spun back round to see that a large jarrah stump had rolled off the stack into what was left of my door. Two gnarly roots like daggers were poking through the window right in front of my face.

Well, I thought, I guess he'll be using his insurance on this one!'

27

Geriatric delinquents

BACK IN DONNYBROOK, THERE were a couple of retirees who used to race around on their mobility scooters. The old boy was a maniac – talk about an (old) boy racer! He was dangerous, screaming around, speeding down the footpath – or what was left of it – and just missing us on purpose. He was an accident waiting to happen.

The old girl, his partner in crime, would ride past on her mobility scooter and abuse us about the state of the pavement, how uneven the ground was, how the temporary wooden ramps going into the shops weren't wide enough (they were) ... and so on.

One morning, I was spreading a bit of sand around for the paving blokes and she came riding down the pavement we had just laid. We'd just ripped out a road crossing and spread some sand, then we'd ramped up the sand about 30 centimetres to meet the new pavement in front of the shops. It was all ready to lay the pavement bricks.

As she approached at her usual breakneck speed, she suddenly screeched to a halt.

Sure enough, she started going off her tree at us. 'I want to go into that shop,' she shouted as she pointed a finger at us, 'but you've darn-well cut me off again!'

I walked over to her and said politely, 'You can just follow the temporary path on the edge of the new road, which is lined with road cones. It's nice and flat. Then just drive up the wooden ramp into the shop. No sweat.'

She gave me a gummy glare. 'Stuff that! I want to use the footpath,' she said, spraying me with spit.

She started to edge forward.

'Look, you can't drive on that,' I said.

'I'll drive where I bloody well like and I'm going up on that new footpath!'

All of a sudden, she sped up.

We stepped out of the way quickly as the old girl racer took a bit of a run-up onto the sand. To my surprise, she made it through the sand on the road crossing.

The front half of her mobility scooter made it up the sand ramp onto the new pavers while the rear end of the scooter got bogged down in the sand – but she didn't give up. Instead, she let rip and opened up the throttle. The little back wheels on her mobility scooter spun furiously, bits of sand flicked off the back wheels, then, to our amazement, the front of the mobility scooter started to rise slowly into the air.

The more she spun the back wheels, the deeper the hole and the more the front of the scooter rose up until it was about to topple over backwards on her. The mobility scooter was near vertical. The old girl's white-knuckled, gnarly old hands were hanging on for dear life and her head was rolled back, staring up at the sky while the long, sparkly tassels at the end of her handlebars fluttered in the wind. The boys ran over and pushed her out, copping abuse as they did it.

That afternoon, the old boy racer sped at us on his mobility scooter and zig-zagged down the street like an idiot. The boys were having to jump out of his way on a daily basis. When he came riding back about an hour later, it was clear that something was wrong. He was crawling along.

'That's not like him,' I said to one of the subbies, as the old-boy racer rode past us looking a bit sheepish. That was when I noticed the huge grass stains on the back of his white shirt. A wipe-out.

* * *

With the new road sealed, pedestrian islands down the middle of the road finished, new street lights down the median strip erected, paving outside the shop fronts almost finished and public relations at an all-time high, the town was starting to take shape. We even got a smile and a 'What a wonderful job you boys are doing,' from one of the shopkeepers.

Some things we had left to do were to fix up the park by the railway station and build two new car parks. As we were digging out the new car park at the southern end of town, I came across the footings of the old turntable that would have been used to turn the steam-train engines around. We also found piles of coal that had been buried there during the steam era.

After work one Friday, we shot into the pub for a drink. It was quite busy, and I recognised a very tall American bloke who the local basketball club had imported to play for them. He walked round the town like he owned it. He used to do odd jobs for the pub.

In the pub, Mr Congeniality walked up and stood right beside me as I was waiting at the bar to be served.

I tried to engage in polite conversation with him and all I got in response was a grunt.

'How're you liking the South West, mate?' I asked.

Grunt.

'How's your basketball doing?' I asked.

Grunt.

I started to wonder whether he could actually talk, when a female backpacker joined us in trying to get to the bar. Well, she got her ear chewed off by him for the next half hour.

When I got back with my drinks to where the boys were sitting, they'd seen the whole thing.

'What a sleaze,' Tim remarked.

'He's been rude to me as well,' Jessie said, glaring at him.

'He thinks he's a bit of a celebrity around here,' Lynchie muttered.

The next day was stinking hot. At lunchtime, I snuck around the back of the Railway Hotel to use their toilets. I hated Portaloos, especially when they'd been baking in the hot sun. Disgusting things. I never used them if I could help it.

Just as I was rounding the corner in a hurry, I bumped into Mr Congeniality. He was wearing paint-spattered overalls and munching on a sandwich.

'Whoops, sorry mate,' I said, as I stepped round him.

I glanced up at his face and burst out laughing. 'Hoy, you're a bit heavy on the old mascara, aren't you mate?'

Mr Congeniality was sporting a big black shiner, which Jessie might have had something to do with.

'Well, I'd love to stay and chat to you, mate, but I need to go somewhere in a hurry,' I added.

'You can't use those toilets, man, if that's where you're thinking of going,' Mr Congeniality said, with a big smirk on his face. 'They're out of order, man. I'm painting them.' And he walked off, probably to finish his lunch.

Busting by now, I glanced at the signs on both doors: 'Out of order.'

'Out of order! Bullshit. It's just a bit of paint. He won't notice if I've been in there or not. The smell will be gone by the time he gets back,' I said to myself.

I shot into one of the toilets and grabbed a seat.

Ah that's better, I thought, as I sat there looking round the cubicle, checking out his handiwork.

'Man, his painting's rough as guts,' I said to myself. I leaned forward to read the graffiti on the inside of the door. 'He's missed that spot completely.'

Crikey, it must have been over 30 degrees in there. I needed some fresh air. I hoisted my pants up and felt around to flush the toilet.

Now, where was the bloody button? I turned around to look for it. Ah, there it was.

My finger disappeared into a round hole in the wall and I had a wiggle around inside. I wiggled a bit more – wiggle, wiggle – feeling for the button. I had a peep through the hole.

Oh! Oh dear! Whoops-a-daisy! The toilet cistern seemed to be missing. Never mind.

I tiptoed out of the toilet and cautiously peered around the door. Good. The coast was clear.

I sneaked off down the laneway, laughing to myself and thinking, wait till I tell the boys.

* * *

The last thing to be done on the Donnybrook job was to put the apple lights back up in the park. The light poles were newly powder-coated and the fibreglass apples had been restored to their former glory. New turf had been rolled out in the park and the place looked awesome.

* * *

It was time for a change of scenery. I got the chance of a lifetime and moved over to England, where I worked driving diggers and dozers all over Warwickshire. I even did a few jobs for lords and ladies on their estates. I worked in an old battlefield, dug up a Roman road, got a good beasting from a retired lady judge while she was riding her horse through her estate – apparently, I'd put a 'beastly hole' in her fence with my digger bucket. The list goes on. Now I've just got to write about it. Cheers for now.

*Also by Mike Bellamy, and available as
an ebook or audiobook*

TOUGH COUNTRY

TALL TALES OF BUSHMEN, BULLDOZERS AND BACK-COUNTRY BLOKES

'It was the mid-1970s and I was about eight, I thought it was completely normal for your old man to pull out a high-powered deer-hunting rifle and fire it through the kitchen door from the breakfast table ...'

In the 1970s and 80s, Barry Bellamy was a fair old bushman, traversing the back-country from Hawke's Bay to the far north in a blue ex-airforce Land Rover. His son Mike would join him as he took up work, wherever he could get it.

Tough Country is Mike's story, about a bygone era of bushmen, scrub-cutters, hunters and shepherds. Later, Mike forged his own life working on the land, and his stories of the characters of the 1980s and 90s, from tradies to digger-drivers, are as hilarious as they are quintessentially Kiwi.